KU-305-319

A NEW HISTORY
OF WALES

JEREMY BLACK

LIVERPOOL LIBRARIES & INFORMATION SERV	
Cypher	22.05.01
942.9/BLA	£8.99
OS ¹¹/₀₆/₀₁	

SUTTON PUBLISHING

First published in the United Kingdom in 2000 by
Sutton Publishing Limited · Phoenix Mill
Thrupp · Stroud · Gloucestershire · GL5 2BU

Copyright © Jeremy Black, 2000

All rights reserved. No part of this publication may be reproduced,
stored in a retrieval system, or transmitted, in any form, or by any
means, electronic, mechanical, photocopying, recording or otherwise,
without the prior permission of the publisher and copyright holder.

Jeremy Black has asserted the moral right to be identified as the
author of this work.

British Library Cataloguing in Publication Data
A catalogue record for this book is available from the British Library

ISBN 0-7509-2320-2

 ALAN SUTTON™ and SUTTON™ are the trade
marks of Sutton Publishing Limited

Typeset in 11/16 pt Photina.
Typesetting and origination by
Sutton Publishing Limited.
Printed and bound in Great Britain by
Cox & Wyman Ltd., Reading, Berkshire.

A NEW HISTORY
OF WALES

- 6 MAR 2017

LV 16973666

Liverpool Libraries

For
David Gwyn

With thanks
for a quarter century of friendship.

CONTENTS

LIST OF MAPS

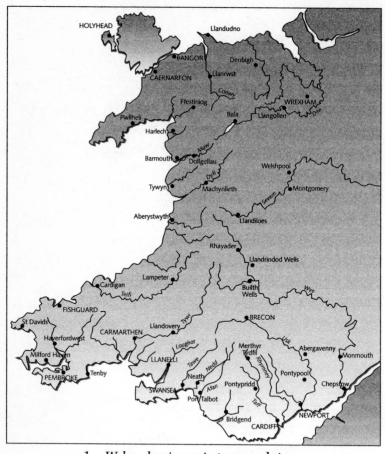

1   *Wales, showing main towns and rivers.*

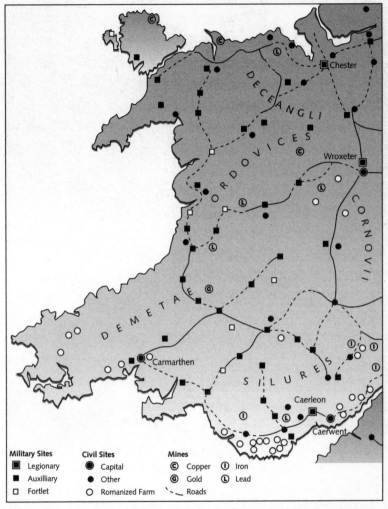

Military Sites
- ▣ Legionary
- ■ Auxilliary
- □ Fortlet

Civil Sites
- ◉ Capital
- ● Other
- ○ Romanized Farm

Mines
- Ⓒ Copper
- Ⓖ Gold
- Ⓘ Iron
- Ⓛ Lead
- ⌐‿⌐ Roads

2. *Roman Wales, showing all known military sites and the principal civilian settlements and Romanised farmsteads. (Cadw: Welsh Historic Monuments. Crown Copyright)*

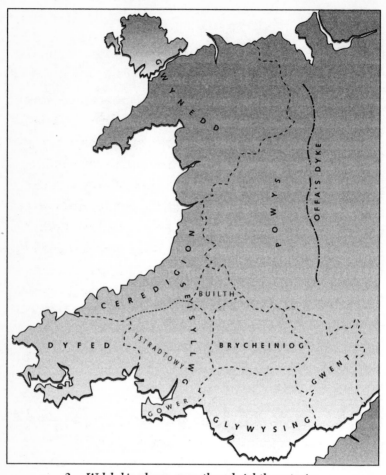

3   *Welsh kingdoms, seventh and eighth centuries.*

PREFACE

Why a new history? For two reasons. First is the decision by a referendum in 1997 to create an assembly for Wales, an assembly that first met in 1999, representing a new beginning that encourages a re-examination of the history of Wales. Secondly, this is a new history of Wales for me, the second I have written. The first, a short essay, was written in 1993 as a sequel to my *History of England* (1993) and as an opportunity to define my ideas before my *History of the British Isles* (1994). It was not published, and when I was given an opportunity in 1999 to write a short history of Wales I decided to start afresh, taking the opportunity to read and think anew rather than trying to revise an earlier text, although I have again sought to do justice to both north and south Wales. Beginning from scratch again brought two other benefits. First, current developments, both in Wales and further afield, encouraged a look at history without earlier pre-conceptions. Secondly, it provided an opportunity to give due weight to the insights offered by recent scholarship.

This at once takes me to acknowledgements. First, the work of other scholars has been of great value. This is accessible not only through books but also through a number of excellent journals, such as that of the National Library of Wales and the *Journal of the Merioneth Historical and Record Society*. Secondly, I benefited from the advice of others on my 1993 and 1999 manuscripts: Tony Carr, Matthew Cragoe, Rees Davies, Stephen Evans, Robin Frame, Bill Gibson, William Griffith, Ralph Griffiths, David Gwyn, Harald Kleinschmidt, Philip Jenkins, Gareth Elwyn Jones, J. Gwynfor Jones, and John R. Kenyon all read sections of one or both. I am also grateful to Tony Pollard and Michael Prestwich for clarifying particular points. Thirdly, I would like to thank Christopher Feeney and Helen Gray of Sutton Publishing for much appreciated assistance. Last, but not least, I thank friends and others who have extended hospitality on my stays in Wales.

LIVERPOOL LIBRARIES &
INFORMATION SERVICES

ONE

WALES BEFORE THE ENGLISH CONQUEST

GEOGRAPHICAL BACKGROUND

The history of a country should first be understood through its geography. To approach Wales from the east across its land frontier or from the west, across the Irish Sea, is to arrive in a country defined by mountains. Wales is not of course the only mountainous part of the British Isles. There are indeed prominent mountain ranges in all of the countries. Furthermore, the Welsh mountains are part of a geological configuration in western Britain. Yet, mountains are more central to Welsh history and identity than is the case with Scotland, let alone England or Ireland. In each of the other countries, especially England and Scotland, state-building centred on lowland areas of relatively prosperous agriculture and relatively high population density.

Wales did not have this option. Wales, understood here as the modern area of Wales, is largely mountainous. Sixty per cent of the surface area is above the 200 metre line. Furthermore, much of lowland Wales is peripheral.

For example, of the traditional counties, the one with the greatest proportion of lowland is the island of Anglesey. Although seen as the granary of Wales, it was scarcely in a position to serve as the basis of Welsh power, not least because, to the south of the Menai Strait, the nearest part of Wales is largely mountainous. There is only a narrow belt of lowland before the mountains of Snowdonia.The peripheral character of the lowlands and the central position of the mountainous watershed ensured that Wales lacked a natural political centre.

The impact of mountains on communications was a central feature of Welsh history, and is still important today. The need to travel up or down added greatly to distance, and thus increased the time and cost of travel. Even in 'lowland' Wales, a small hill often affected road and rail routes. Furthermore, many mountains were difficult to cross. It was not until the nineteenth century that advances in transport engineering, especially bridge-building and the use of dynamite, nitro-glycerine and gelignite in tunnel construction, helped overcome some of the problems posed by the terrain. Even so, there were few long tunnels in Wales, unlike in England.

Furthermore, the configuration of the mountains affected Welsh history, not least by making north–south communications more difficult than west–east. This put a premium on land links with England, for example along the north and south coasts to Chester and Gloucester respectively. The configuration of the mountains also ensured that sea routes were important but, again, these did not contribute to the unity of Wales. Coastal links were essentially between north Wales and Chester or Liverpool, west Wales and Ireland, and south Wales and other ports in the Bristol Channel, rather than between the coastal parts of Wales. The terrain affected settlement patterns as well as communications, the two of course being linked.

The impact of the mountains was important not only in terms of the geography of Wales as a whole, but also with reference to particular parts of it. Thus in north-west Wales the flat alluvial floor of the Conwy valley to the east of Snowdonia was important as a north–south route and as a centre for control in the region.

The slopes of mountainous and hilly regions were difficult to cultivate and limited the land available for settlement. The slopes were also affected by high rainfall. The prevailing westerly winds ensure that rainfall is related to relief; coming off the sea, they are, also, salt-laden as well as strong, which affects growth near the coast. Anglesey, the lowest county, is the driest, mostly receiving between 35 and 40 inches of rain a year. The

Conwy valley has a similar figure, but in Snowdonia there are much higher totals, with much of the mountainous area receiving over 80 inches a year. The combination of heavy rainfall and high run-off from steep slopes ensured that valley bottoms were often affected by rivers and streams in spate. This had an impact on agriculture, settlement and communications. The period of rainfall also posed problems: for example, heavy August rains hit wheat cultivation.

Furthermore, these are averages. Farmers had and have to take note of variations not only in rainfall but also in the length of the frost-free season, a length that again is closely related to relief. Thus, southern Pembrokeshire, where long periods of frost and snow are very rare, has an earlier growing season than most of Wales, and, as a result, was able to produce early potatoes for distant markets in the twentieth century. In addition, much of the rain in upland areas falls as drizzle and there are prolonged cloud conditions. Cloud, mist and drizzle restrict sunlight and thus lessen the growing season.

Over the centuries, heavy rainfall has helped wash soil from the uplands. This ensures that much of Wales has poor, frequently acidic, soils. This lessens its suitability for continuous or intensive cultivation, particularly in the absence of fertilisers. There has also been a serious

problem with poor drainage. Seventeenth-century sur-
veyors frequently classified land as 'heath and furze' or
'rocky, stony ground'. Modern Agricultural Land
Classification maps are less eloquent but similarly bleak.
For example, that for Anglesey in 1962 recorded no
Grade 1 farming and only 5½ square miles of Grade 2.
Anglesey provides a good example of the mistake of
assuming that poor soils are only found in upland areas.
Many lowland areas were also affected by erosion,
especially that of glaciation.

The combination of poor soils, steep slopes, a limited
growing season and high relief encouraged dependence
on the rearing of animals. In steep areas this meant
sheep, in flatter regions cattle. Neither, especially sheep-
rearing, offered a form of agriculture that could support
the population levels of arable regions or encouraged
nucleated (village) settlement. Instead, dispersed settlement was the norm, frequently in the form of isolated
farmsteads. This was also true of areas that, thanks to
the climate and soil, were most suitable for woodland,
such as much of Montgomeryshire.

These areas of poor terrain separated the more fertile
lands in a way that was not matched in England, or
indeed in the broad swathe of fertile lowland in central
and north-east Scotland: Ayr to Aberdeen. In Wales,

there was of course good land although the quality of some of the lowland had been affected by glacial erosion, for example in Anglesey. The limited amount of good land both there and along the northern coast, especially in the Vale of Clwyd in Denbighshire in the north-east, is overshadowed by the far more extensive good land to the south of the main massif: southern Pembrokeshire, the Vale of Glamorgan, and the Vale of Aeron in Cardiganshire, with its large dairy farms. The Vale of Glamorgan and other parts of south Wales also benefit from higher temperatures, while to the lee (east) of Pembrokeshire, rainfall figures are lower than in the north and the growing season is longer.

These coastal regions were to play a central role in the history of Wales, eventually coming to dominate the demographics, society and economy of the country. Yet, in an agricultural age, it was rather the contrast between say Radnor and the better farming land of Herefordshire in the neighbouring part of England that was important. Taking Wales as a whole, relatively low population levels and a poorly-developed agricultural base ensured that there was only a modest surplus of wealth for taxation – by rulers, churches and landlords – and thus only a limited ability to support political and governmental activity, again in comparison with that of England. It is necessary to be cautious not to extrapolate modern conditions into the past. The climate was not constant, and it is clear that cereal cultivation across much of Wales was possible. However, England did not have a central mountainous watershed limiting unity.

BEFORE THE ROMANS

Settlement long preceded agriculture. Neanderthal hunters visited Wales, and the earliest known human remains yet found in Wales – part of a jaw, including teeth, dated about 230,000 BC – has recently been found in Pontnewydd cave. This is one of the most northerly discoveries of hominid remains. Human activity in Old Stone Age Wales was probably limited by the impact of successive advances of glacial ice. With time, the human record improves. The 'Red Lady of Paviland', in fact a young male buried in about 25,000 BC in Paviland cave on the Gower peninsula, was found with evidence of a ceremonial burial, including perforated sea shells and mammoth-ivory adornments.

The maximum advance of the ice, in about 20–18,000 BC, made Wales uninhabitable, but, after its last retreat in about 10,000 BC, human occupation became permanent, helped by a warmer climate. The people of the Middle Stone Age, about 8500–4500 BC, exploited the now wooded landscape by hunting animals and gathering berries, a system of land use that did little damage to the environment, but one that was only compatible with a low density of population.

Farming began with the New Stone Age in around 4000 BC. Polished stone axes were used to clear trees, and their production led to trade as these axes were only produced on some sites. Farming led to permanent settlement and more developed communal life. The latter is indicated by communal graves, the largest at Tinkinswood in Glamorgan, and, from about 3000 BC, standing stone alignments and circles, as at Penrhos Feilw on Holyhead Island. Both represented much collective effort and were the focus of agrarian society.

From about 2500 BC burial practices changed, with individual graves in round barrows becoming more important. This has been linked to a socio-political change, specifically a decline of community and the dominance of society by powerful individuals, who can be described as chieftains or aristocrats. The metal-working of the Bronze Age was established from about 2000 BC.

Socio-political developments interacted with ecological changes in about 1400–1200 BC. As the weather became colder and the deforested uplands ceased to be cultivatable, a major and lasting shift in the Welsh environment, there was increased pressure on the lowland farmland, and society became more warlike. This in turn encouraged the role of chieftains and other warriors. The role of conflict in Iron Age Wales, which began in about 600 BC, is indicated by surviving weapons and by approximately 600 hillforts from the period. The latter were a testimony to territorialisation, the control of particular territories or distinct tribes.

Nevertheless, pre-Roman Wales was less 'developed' than southern England, without the latter's coinage, proto-towns, and 'states' with monarchical patterns of government. Most of late Iron Age Wales, for example, left no trace of pottery. Yet that does not imply limited settlement. To take Caernarvonshire, there are numerous Stone Age sites and the megalithic monuments indicate not only coastal settlements but also movement into suitable inland areas, such as the Llŷn peninsula, much of which is a lowland plateau. In the Bronze Age (2000–500 BC), the search for metal ores in Snowdonia further encouraged penetration into the interior. Anglesey became a major centre of trade, including to southern England and Ireland. By the Iron Age (600 BC–AD 100), there were numerous hill forts in Caernarvonshire, both bank-and-ditch and stone-walled. Over fifty have been found, although they were not occupied simultaneously.

The Celtic population of Wales was divided into a number of tribes that seem to have been grouped together into confederations. Cornovii, Deceangli Demetae, Ordovices and Silures are the Celtic names these tribes conferred on themselves or on each other. They were Latinised slightly to fit into the Latin case-system. The Silures were in Glamorgan, the Demetae in Pembrokeshire, the Ordovices in Snowdonia, the Deceangli in Clwyd, and the Cornovii in the upper valley of the Severn. Although the units were not co-terminous, this looked toward the later division of Wales into south-east, south-west, north-west and north-east, and both were a consequence of the centrifugal impact of the mountainous core. The largest surviving known hillforts were to the east of central Wales, in what is now good farmland in Shropshire and Herefordshire. Some were larger than 20 acres, and that at Llanymynech, between Welshpool and Oswestry, was 140 acres.

ROMAN CONQUEST

The initial Roman invasions of England under Julius Caesar in 55 and 54 BC had had no direct impact on Wales which, unlike southern England, was not involved in the struggle between the Romans and the Gauls of modern France. The more serious and, as it turned out, lasting invasion launched by the Emperor Claudius in AD 43, again of south-east England, also did not affect Wales, but the situation changed rapidly. Caratacus, the leader of the Catuvellauni, who had headed the resistance in south-east England, fled to Wales after the south-east was conquered, and became influential there, although how far so is unclear. Ostorius Scapula, who took over as Governor in AD 47, was determined to consolidate the Roman success in southern England and the Midlands by dealing with Caratacus and Wales. Probably in AD 48, he moved against the Deceangli in north-east Wales, but, after initial success, drew back out of concern about the attitude of the Brigantes in northern England. In about AD 49, the XX Legion was moved from Colchester to Kingsholm, Gloucester, and then used by Scapula to operate against the Silures and to defeat Caratacus. Although there has been much controversy about the site, it has been suggested that Caratacus was defeated at Llanymynech. He then fled to Queen Cartimandua of the Brigantes who handed him over to the Romans.

Wales was not easy to campaign in and it is likely that Scapula's forces did not move far into modern Wales. The garrisons he based in south-east Wales came under serious pressure from the Silures who inflicted a number of defeats. Scapula died in AD 52 and his successor,

Didius Gallus (AD 52–7), stabilised the situation, but without pressing forward. The Emperor Nero had thought of abandoning Britain. It is interesting to consider how different the history of Wales would have been had the Romans done so, and this is a reminder of the role of chance in history. In fact, Scapula's replacement, Quintus Veranius (AD 57), was put in to resume the advance. He was not interested in building forts and, instead, mounted a swift attack on the Silures before dying.

Veranius was replaced by Suetonius Paulinus who again devoted himself to expansion into Wales, not northern England. After campaigning in south and north Wales, he launched an amphibious attack on Anglesey in AD 60. This was both a major centre of Druid rites and a refuge for those fleeing the Romans. Paulinus' attack was successful, and the Druids' sacred groves were destroyed, but, before he could consolidate the position, Paulinus had to turn to deal with the serious rising led by Boudica of the Iceni. Thereafter, Wales was ignored while the Roman position was re-established in southern England. After that, troops were moved to fight the Parthians of what is modern Iran. In AD 69–73 the Romans concentrated within Britain on subjugating the Brigantes, but in AD 73/4–6 a new governor, Julius Frontinus, conquered most of Wales. Very little is known about these campaigns, which were accompanied by extensive fort-building. The conquest was completed under the governorship of Julius Agricola (AD 77/8–83/4). He arrived to find the Ordovicians in rebellion, but rapidly subdued them and established the Roman position both in Snowdonia and in Anglesey. All of Wales had been conquered, the first time that it had been united; although not of course as Wales but, rather, within two separate provinces of Britannia.

ROMAN RULE

The conquest was followed by the standard features of Roman imperial rule. Wales was not a special case, nor a long-term problem. An extensive network of about thirty-five fortresses was constructed and they were linked by roads to legionary bases at Deva (Chester) and Isca (Caerleon), the latter the headquarters of the II Legion from AD 75 until about AD 290. This system was designed to enforce pacification in what was a military zone and reflected the extent to which the conquest of Wales had been more difficult than that of south-west England.

Yet it is important not to exaggerate the strength of the military presence. There is no evidence of Roman bases on the mainland further west than Segontium

(Caernarfon), where there was a Mithraic temple for the garrison, and Moridunum (Carmarthen), and the Roman presence in Cardiganshire was limited. The watchtower or signal station built on Holyhead mountain in Anglesey was designed to serve against raiders from Ireland rather than in order to hold down the island. Indeed the base there was not built until the end of the third century, or later.

The security system in Wales was rapidly reduced, in part because the country became quiet and in part because the situation in Scotland was more serious. Although there is evidence that there was some unrest in Wales in the second century, the garrison was smaller than that in northern Britain. There is evidence of the abandonment of some forts in about AD 100. The Celtic leadership was deliberately Romanised – urged to follow Roman ways and, in many cases, live in towns. Towns were established on the Roman pattern, both next to fortresses, as at Caerleon and Segontium; and separate to the military presence, as at Caerwent, which was developed as a tribal capital for the Silures. Wales was important to the Roman economy, producing copper, lead, iron and gold. Pre-Roman use of mineral resources had been limited, although recent archaeological work has established Bronze Age mining in north and mid-Wales.

Furthermore, the gold mines at Dolaucothi in Cardiganshire had possibly been exploited. Nevertheless, as radiocarbon dating has pushed back the dates of some sites from the Romans to the Bronze Age, it is now evident that there was major expansion under the Romans. This was true at Dolaucothi, in the mining of lead at Halkyn and Draethen, and possibly of copper at Parys. Iron was mined in the Forest of Dean. A procurator, in charge of imperial mining, probably had his residence in the fort at Segontium. Mineral rights were an imperial monopoly, and the development of mining in Wales made it important to the Roman state. Mining may also have brought some native prosperity. The number of coin-hoards in Caernarvonshire, where copper was mined, has been seen in this light. There is also evidence of prosperity in Anglesey, another copper-working region, in the third and fourth centuries.

Nevertheless, aside from the mineral-linked presence, Wales was not an area of marked Romanisation. There were, for example, few towns or villas, and Romanisation was especially weak in west and north Wales. As such, Wales shared the fate of the upland areas outside southern Britain with the major additional factor that there was no significant military presence.

When the role of the military was emphasised anew in

the mid-fourth century, this was in response not to rebellion from within Wales but rather to a threat from abroad that faced both Roman rule and the native population. 'Barbarian' attacks from across the Irish Sea led to coastal defensive works, as at Cardiff and Caerwent, and to a reinforcement of the garrison at Segontium. Irish tribes indeed appear to have settled in west and north Wales in the fifth century.

In the late fourth century, the Roman presence lessened considerably. Far from concentrating on the defence of the empire, Roman forces were withdrawn in order to support the imperial quest of their generals on the Continent. One such, Magnus Maximus, who claimed the empire in AD 383, was presented in the medieval Welsh legend *Breuddwyd Macsen Wledig* as Macsen Wledig, founder of a number of major lineages. This was designed to support the pretensions of the dynasty of Gwynedd, but later studies have shown this to be unfounded. Such a desire for continuity was to be important in the historical myths of many medieval European dynasties, but in the case of Wales there was particularly little to lay claim to. Direct Roman rule ceased in the first decade of the fifth century.

Nevertheless, Roman 'magic' persisted: the long shadow cast by the Roman empire was seen as the fount of legitimate political authority long after its fall. Welsh rulers established their courts on Roman sites and some claimed descent from Magnus Maximus for that reason. This Roman magic also lay behind Geoffrey of Monmouth's *Historia Regum Britanniae* (1135) in which he alleged a Trojan descent for the Britons as for the Romans.

INDEPENDENT WALES BEFORE THE NORMAN CHALLENGE

The post-Roman history of Britain is obscure. Written sources are few, although not that few compared to those of other parts of Britain and the Continent as well. There are many fairly early saints' lives which can be scrutinised on a number of topics. Nevertheless, much is not covered; the legends, such as that about King Arthur, are opaque, and the archaeological evidence is limited and sometimes ambiguous. The fifth century is particularly obscure and this is very much the case with Wales. It ceased to be part of a major empire, with the opportunities for reports and record-keeping that that offered, and instead became a congeries of political units focusing on the essential tribal leadership of locally powerful warlords. This was not the best basis for the continuation of the Roman system. Urban activity continued in Caerleon and possibly Carmarthen, and Roman estate units may have continued to function in south-east Wales, but the Romanisation of the elite faded rapidly. They used Roman titles, such as magistrate, but these now meant little. Instead, with the decline of town life, the elite returned to their pre-Roman basis, living in hillforts and using them as the foci of their power. Obscure figures such as Maelgwn, ruler of Gwynedd (d. 547), should be seen as tribal warlords.

Trade links by sea, however, remained important and helped to link Wales to the wider world. There was a thriving trade between south Wales and places as far distant as Sicily with goods including glassware and ceramics. The owners of the fortified hilltop at Dinas Powys near Cardiff, occupied from the late fifth to seventh centuries, possibly the rulers of the principality of Glywysing, had wine from the Mediterranean and other goods from France.

Trade routes with Ireland were especially important, and this served not only for trade but also for settlement from Ireland and for the expansion of Christianity. The development and extent of Christianity under the Romans is obscure, and it was probably not widespread. There is some evidence for practice in the south-east, the most Christianised part of Wales, and Christianity was part of the Roman legacy, at least in the upper levels of society. Yet there is scant sign of a 'trickle down' effect in Wales.

In the late fifth century, however, missionary activity from Gaul (France) began. Irish missionaries were also important. Illtud from Brittany, the Celtic part of France, established a school and a monastery, probably at Llanilltud Fawr (Glamorgan), and both were centres for missionary activity. St David, the son of Nou, a Welsh woman, was active in Dyfed, which was exposed to religious influences from both Ireland and Continental Europe. At Llandewi Brefi, St David is claimed to have confronted the devil. He founded St Davids and, from there, churches across south Wales.

Missionaries established both monasteries and smaller church settlements, such as St Seiriol's monastery on Ynys Lannog in Anglesey, and small hermitages. They moved along the coasts and many of the early churches were on or close to them. Missionaries such as St Beuno in Gwynedd and St Cadoc in south-east Wales, the son of an early ruler of Glamorgan, and St Cybi in Anglesey, were honoured as holy men, and churches were dedicated to them. Islands off the coast, such as Bardsey and Holyhead, were especially favoured as religious sites. As saints were frequently buried on islands they also became pilgrimage sites.

Christianity was a major force in post-Roman Wales, but one that is possibly disproportionately important in the surviving record. Nevertheless, there is evidence of ecclesiastical sites from all over Wales, and Christianity provided a measure of cultural coherence. Latin was used for liturgical purposes and for inscriptions and gravestones. Christian France was an influence common to most of the early memorial inscriptions in Wales, and the use of Latin helped to affirm its value and prestige.

Nevertheless, the Celtic language of the pre-Roman and Roman periods survived as an active vernacular. It was in this period that a branch of a Celtic language evolved into Welsh, Strathclyde/Cumbrian, Cornish and Breton; this can be traced in some of the surviving inscriptions. The remains of the visual arts from this period are scanty, but the interlaced patterns of the wheel-crosses, such as that at Nevern in Pembrokeshire, indicate that the 'Celtic' culture of Wales was shared with other areas of Britain not conquered by the Anglo-Saxons. In Wales, an older language, and thus culture, survived both the Romans and the Anglo-Saxon invasions of Britain that began in the fifth century.

To use the term Wales, or indeed England, for this period is of course anachronistic. Wales was not yet a distinct area or culture. This can be illustrated by considering Welsh poetry, the survival of which is seen as starting with Taliesin and Aneirin in the sixth century. Taliesin wrote a series of poems in praise of Urien of Rheged and his son Owain, but Rheged was a principality near Carlisle. Aneirin's poem described his lord, Mynyddog Mwyn-fawr of Edinburgh. This indicates the difficulty of associating early 'Welsh' culture with the geographical area of Wales. Instead, Welsh was a fragment from the older British civilization that the Anglo-Saxons shattered.

The conflict with the Anglo-Saxons defined Wales culturally, ethnically and politically; a frequent situation in post-Roman Europe, as peoples defined themselves following the collapse of the concept of unity under Roman rule. Wales was given identity by the conquerors in terms of otherness: the Saxons used *Walas* or *Wealas* to describe the Britons, and it meant both serfs and foreigners. As the Angles and Saxons advanced westward from the North Sea coasts, links between the surviving Romano-British communities were broken. Strathclyde, Wales and Cornwall failed to offer effective long-term resistance and were thus separated, at least by land.

The early stages of the struggle are obscure but, in the early seventh century, the Anglian kingdom of Northumbria and the rulers of north Wales competed for control of north England. In 615, Ethelfrith of North-umbria conquered Cheshire, killing Selyf ap Cynan, the ruler of Powys, in battle near Chester. The pagan Ethelfrith also killed many of the monks of Bangor Is-coed (Bangor on Dee), who had prayed for his defeat. The loss of Cheshire was important, for this was one of the more extensive fertile parts of 'Wales' north of the Vale of Glamorgan. It also linked Wales and the Britons west of the Pennines.

Ethelfrith's successor, Edwin (617–33), continued Northumbrian pressure on the Welsh, defeating Cad-wallon of Gwynedd in 629 and capturing Anglesey. Cadwallon, a Christian, then allied with the pagan Penda, ruler of the Anglian kingdom of Mercia. In 633, they invaded Northumbria, defeating and killing Edwin at Heathfield in what is modern south Yorkshire. Cadwallon was, in turn, defeated and killed by Edwin's nephew, Oswald, the following year at Rowley Burn near Hexham, and the Welsh lost their links with the Cumbrians. Those with the Celts of south-west England had already been lost as a result of the Saxon victory at Dyrham (577), after which Gloucestershire was taken, although the battle is a subject of debate. It is unclear that it was fought by 'Saxon' troops, as the Anglian chronicler Bede (c. 672–735) insists: the Gewisse, the emerging rulers in

Wessex, might not have been Saxons. Further north, Cynddylan, the last Welsh ruler of what is now Shropshire, had been killed. The struggle between Mercia and Northumbria dominated the period 630–800. It was won by Mercia, not by any of the British kingdoms. Indeed, the latter had played a role essentially as adjuncts.

Wales became the most important area of surviving Romano-British civilisation. It is unclear how far this led to a sense of cultural identity and pride, but evidence of a sense of continuity was provided by the *Historia Brittonum* (*History of the Britons*) possibly compiled in about 796 by 'Nennius', a monk from central Wales. However, almost everything is controversial about this group of texts, most notably to what extent the several versions existing under this label can be construed to go back to one archetype.

Pressure from the English east shaped the extent of Wales. The Angles of Mercia conquered the valley of the Severn, and then Herefordshire in the mid-seventh century. The last was a major loss. Herefordshire had been similar to other lowland areas peripheral to the mountainous core of Wales, and was a natural sphere of expansion from it. Control over Herefordshire was to be contested into the eleventh century. It had been conquered by the Magonsaete, a tribe that was brought under the control of the ruler of Mercia. Whether the Magonsaete were Anglians, as Bede insisted, is difficult to determine.

Meanwhile, Offa, King of Mercia 757–96, in about 784–96 had created a frontier line – the ditched rampart known as Offa's Dyke – running from the Severn estuary to the Dee, that may well have been a defensive work. It was built after the Welsh attack in 784. It has also been argued that the Dyke was essentially a boundary, not a defensive line, and that it may have arisen from an agreed frontier. At least some sections of the Dyke, however, probably had a defensive function. Offa's Dyke was to mark the definition of a border and of Wales and England. Nowhere else in the British Isles was a frontier quite so crucial. The building of this earth dyke was not the end of Mercian expansion. In 822 Offa's successor, Cenwulf, invaded northern Wales, destroyed the fortress of Deganwy on the Conwy, and annexed Powys. Dyfed was also attacked in his reign.

This pressure was to abate, thanks first to the rise in the 820s of the Saxon kingdom of Wessex, for which, with its focus on southern England, expansion against Wales was of scant importance, and secondly to the impact of the Vikings. Although there were serious Viking attacks on Wales, they did not compare to the campaigns of conquest in ninth- and early eleventh-century England.

Even without these developments, however, it would be mistaken to present Welsh history in this period solely in terms of resistance to English attack. Important as that was, it neglects the role of internecine struggles and runs the risk of falsely juxtaposing overly-coherent realities of Welshness and Englishness.

Wales was divided into a number of small kingdoms, or *gwledydd*. Within each, below the ruling group, society was divided between free men and unfree or bondmen; the latter worked the land. As in England, the tendency from the sixth century on was for a decline in the number of kingdoms, as the less successful, such as Gower, Gwent, Ergyng, Ceredigion, Builth, Brycheiniog, and Powys, were taken over. Thus, in the eighth century Ystrad Tywi was taken over by Ceredigion to its north, the two forming the kingdom of Seisyllwg. The most expansive were Gwynedd in the north-west, Dyfed in the south-west and Glywysing in the south-east. They were the kingdoms based on the largest amount of fertile lowland; but, in addition, they benefited from a degree of immunity from the English. In contrast, Powys in the north-east suffered considerably at the hands of Mercia, while English pressure may also have been responsible in part for the demise of the kingdoms in the upper Wye. In 916, an English raiding force destroyed the Llangorse

Crannog, an artificial island in Llangorse lake, that had been built for the King of Brycheiniog in about 900.

Powys extended into Cheshire, Shropshire and Herefordshire, but these territories were lost. This weakened Powys, contributing to the loss of the southernmost part of Powys: Rhwrng Gwy a Hafren (between Wye and Severn) passed to a branch of the dynasty. In short, a principality that might have served as the base for a strong state between the mountains and the Severn, one that could have reached from the north coast to the Wye, was gravely weakened by external pressure.

Nevertheless, it was not simply a case of the English setting the terms for Welsh political development. The failure of Ceredigion and Gwrtheyrnion in central Wales to survive was due in part to the greater strength of Gwynedd and Dyfed, a strength that, in part, reflected the centrifugal consequences of the relative wealth of coastal Wales and the poverty of central Wales. The exact bounds of Gwynedd are unclear, and such a concept anyway is of limited value. However, Gwynedd included Anglesey and probably extended beyond the river Clwyd, although its position there was contested both by Mercia and by Powys.

Gwynedd was the basis of the power of Rhodri Mawr (d. 878), who claimed descent from Magnus Maximus and the sixth-century ruler of Gwynedd, Maelgwn; but he also ruled much of central Wales including Powys, which he inherited from his uncle in 855, and Seisyllwg which he took over in 871 when his brother-in-law, the ruler, died. Rhodri had to confront the growing power of the Vikings, who began pressing on the north Welsh coast, especially Anglesey, from the 850s. They defeated Rhodri Mawr in the 'Sunday Battle' in Anglesey in 867, forcing him to flee to Ireland.

Later Viking attacks were mounted in 903, 961, when Holyhead was plundered, and 971, when the monastery of Penmon on the Anglesey coast was plundered, 972, 980, 987, when 2,000 prisoners were taken from Anglesey for sale as slaves in Ireland, and 993. The Vikings plundered Aberffraw, the royal seat of Gwynedd, close to the coast of Anglesey, in 968. It is possible that the Vikings had suzerainty over Gwynedd at the end of the tenth century and the beginning of the eleventh. The Viking impact, nevertheless, was far less than on England and Ireland, in part because Wales was poorer and less attractive for raiding and settlement. However, the legacy of Viking place names, such as Anglesey and Swansea (Sweynsey), suggests that, as elsewhere, the Vikings came to trade and settle, as well as devastate. Rhodri also fought the Mercians, and was killed when they invaded in 878. This increased the attraction of appealing for support to Wessex. However, Mercia was soon after effectively partitioned between Wessex and the Danelaw. To both, Wales was a side issue.

Welsh inheritance customs – the division of property among sons – may have made it difficult to translate territorial gains into more cohesive statehood, although kingship was indivisible, and the frequent conflicts of the period put a premium on successful military leadership. What probably happened in the case of such rulers as Rhodri Mawr was that they might accumulate several kingships and, on their deaths, individual ones would be inherited by individual sons. Rhodri's son Anarawad succeeded to Gwynedd and another son, Cadell, to Seisyllwg.

Rhodri's grandson, Hywel Dda, Howel the Good (d. 950), son of Cadell, initially succeeded only to Ceredigion, although he came to rule most of Wales, more so than Rhodri. He added Dyfed by marriage in about 905, and seized Gwynedd and Powys in about 942. Hywel was a major figure, the first Welsh king who certainly issued his own coinage, and in about 928 he went on pilgrimage to Rome. Although the surviving documents date from far later, Hywel is also held to have been the codifier of Welsh law; though this may be a twelfth-century appeal to history. The laws attributed to him, which were allegedly codified in an assembly at Tŷ Gwyn ar Dâf (Whitland), were the basis of an ordered kindred society down to 1284 in some respects and to 1536 in others.

Hywel's death was followed by the collapse of his realm and internecine conflict, especially the recovery of independence by Gwynedd. The Old English state that had developed from Wessex, with its growing pretensions to overlordship in Britain, came to intervene in Wales with increasing frequency. The political geography of Wales may be compared with that of England; kingship was inherent in the individual kingdoms and there was no kingship of Wales. But in England unity was created by the destruction of all the kingships save that of Wessex in the ninth century by the Vikings. This did not happen in Wales and a similar process of consolidation in the face of foreign attack was delayed until the Anglo-Normans conquered much of Wales. The south Welsh made some kind of submission to Alfred, King of Wessex, to whom they turned for help against the Vikings, in 886, and this may have lasted into the early tenth century. Welsh rulers attended the court of Alfred's grandson Athelstan (924–39), who had imperial ambitions, Hywel subscribing to charters drawn up by Athelstan's *witan* (aristocratic council). These princes were clearly regarded by the English as Athelstan's subordinates (*subreguli*), and Athelstan exacted tribute. It is possibly from this period that the *Armes Prydein* (*Prophecy of Britain*), a poem calling for Welsh unity and the expulsion of the English from Britain, dates. The poem promised that the Welsh would be aided by St David and other non-English peoples, including the Cornish, Bretons, Irish and Strathclyde Britons.

The princes of Wales did not take part in the submission to Alfred's son, Edward, made by the rulers of Scotland, Danish York and the Strathclyde Britons in 920, but a Welsh ruler seems to have taken part in the ceremony by which King Edgar was rowed in a boat by subordinate rulers at Chester in 973. Under both Athelstan and Edward the Confessor (1042–66), the royal titles of King of the English and of Britain were used indifferently, and, although Ireland was completely independent, Wales and Scotland were in part dependent.

The Welsh rulers of the period spent much of their time in conflict. Hywel's grandson, Maredudd ab Owain (986–99) of Dyfed, attacked his Welsh neighbours and fought the Danes. He regained Gwynedd and Powys. However, after his death, Gwynedd again regained independence, beginning a volatile period in which rulers were displaced by powerful figures. This was especially the case in Gwynedd where in 1018 Llywelyn ap Seisyll, Maredudd's son-in-law, seized control. He died in 1023, before he could consolidate his position, but – like Rhodri Mawr (with the exception of Dyfed), Hywel Dda, and Maredudd – ruled both north and west Wales, suggesting that their short-term union was possible for a powerful ruler. This broke up on Llywelyn's death, when Gwynedd was brought again under its legitimate line, but in 1039 Llywelyn's son, Gruffydd ap Llywelyn, took Gwynedd. In 1044, he conquered Deheubarth, the kingdom that then included Dyfed, Brycheiniog and Seisyllwg. The rise of Gwynedd in the eleventh century under Llywelyn ab Seisyll and Gruffydd ap Llywelyn (d. 1063) was the most important development in the pre-Norman period. Both Llywelyn and Gruffydd had to fight to gain control of Gwynedd and both campaigned in south Wales, most of which was conquered between 1039 and 1060. Gwent and Morgannwg were both conquered in the 1050s. Gruffydd can be seen as the sole native Prince to rule all of Wales. The length of the process reflected the difficulty of obtaining a decisive 'political' settlement short of slaying rivals, as Gruffydd twice did.

Matters were also complicated by foreign intervention: the Dublin Norse, the Vikings established in Dublin, assisted Gruffydd's opponents, but Welsh rulers were ready to seek such aid, Gruffydd himself gaining the help of Earl Godwin of Wessex's son Swein in 1046. However, he also had serious clashes with the English. After a successful attack in 1039, Gruffydd ravaged Herefordshire in 1052, 1054 and 1056. It was an area of particular tension where the English were expanding to the west of Offa's Dyke. Gruffydd was a threat to the ambitions of Harold Godwinson of Wessex, because of his alliance with Earl Aelfgar of Mercia and the political implications of that alliance. War resumed in 1062, but Gruffydd found Harold a formidable foe. In 1062, he burnt Gruffydd's palace at Rhuddlan. In 1063, Harold, campaigning by land and sea, harried Wales, advancing as far as Snowdonia. Gruffydd was deserted by the lesser rulers before being killed by some of his men, his head being delivered to Harold, who also took his wife. Gruffydd's half-brothers were allowed to inherit Gwynedd on condition they swore allegiance.

It is unclear whether Gwynedd could have developed as Wessex did in the tenth and eleventh centuries, serving as the basis for a Welsh state. Unlike in the Old-English state, there is little sign of administrative sophistication, but that is also true of Scotland in this period. Furthermore, Scotland was also divided, most obviously with a kingdom centred on the Moray Firth resisting control until the early twelfth century. The 'conquest' of one part of Wales by the ruler of another amounted to submission and hostages rather than territorial control. What is clear is that the power of the rulers of Gwynedd rested on military success. The primacy of military power remained the case, and after the Norman conquest of England the pressure on Wales increased.

This account of war should not be taken to imply that the history of Wales in the period between the departure of the Romans and the arrival of the Normans was simply one of violence, let alone anarchic violence. There were also important long-term trends, one of which – the consolidation of authority – was indeed linked to conflict. More generally, the period was one of an increased establishment and territorialisation of church and state. This was a matter not only of the foundation of sites but also of a measure of institutionalisation, as with the foundation of administrative units within *gwlads* or states. These were first *cantrefi* and then their subdivisions *cymydau*. The latter were important for law and taxation, more specifically the organisation of courts and the collection of dues, both facets of the 'vertical' character of government. In turn, this process became more stable as peripatetic rulership declined in favour of fixed centres of authority. In the former case, rulers literally ate the taxes, in the form of food dues. In the latter, taxation became more important. This amounted to a development not only in government but also in society and the economy, for monetarisation and the spread of a money economy encouraged a greater responsiveness to the wider world. However, the distinction between freemen and bondmen continued.

THE CONQUEST

In the eleventh and twelfth centuries Wales did not follow England in being rapidly overrun by the Normans, in contrast to the situation under the Romans. Instead, Wales was more like Scotland under the Romans: conquered only in part. William the Conqueror (1066–87) was not interested in the conquest of Wales, which did not exist as a political unit anyway. He saw himself as the legitimate heir of the West Saxon dynasty and therefore as the inheritor of that dynasty's relationship with its Welsh and Scottish neighbours. What William and his successors probably sought in Wales was stability, and this may explain William's agreement with Rhys ap Tewdwr, ruler of of Deheubarth, the principality in south-west Wales. What royal campaigns there were in Wales were not aimed at conquest; there was always a specific and limited objective. The Norman rulers were more concerned, first, with Danish attacks on, and rebellion within, England and, secondly, with conflict in Normandy and with France.

William I sought to anchor the frontier by creating three powerful earldoms, Chester, Shrewsbury and Hereford. Their position, however, was not solely defensive. Both the Earls and their followers sought to expand into Wales, which was newly vulnerable after the death of Gruffydd ap Llywelyn in 1063 and the subsequent disunity.

Conquest in Wales in the late eleventh century was of individual kingdoms or political units by individual Norman adventurers: this was a land of opportunity for aggressive and land-hungry younger sons, although some of the most significant early Normans, such as Roger of Montgomery, Earl of Shrewsbury, and William fitz Osbern, Earl of Hereford, were leading court magnates. In one case, that of Glamorgan, a whole over-kingdom in all its political complexity was conquered. Robert of Rhuddlan tried to do the same in 1081 when he captured Gruffydd ap Cynan of Gwynedd, but Robert was swiftly killed. Further south, Philip de Braose seized Radnor in about 1090 and then established himself in Builth, while

Bernard de Newmarch took over Brycheiniog, establishing a castle at Brecon. Rhys ap Tewdwr was killed resisting this expansion. These Normans were operating outside the kingdom of England; they were not under the direct auspices of the king. However, they would not touch a ruler who had a formal agreement with the king. Instead, they tended to move in when there was a vacancy or a disputed succession.

Initially, the Normans advanced with great momentum, across the lowerland on the eastern borders of Wales, along the lowlands near the south and north coasts, and up the river valleys. William fitz Osbern built a stone castle, the first in Wales, at Chepstow in 1067–71, and used it as a base for expansion; he founded the lordship of Strigoil in southern Gwent. Roger of Montgomery founded a castle of Montgomery and advanced from there along the valley of the upper Severn into Central Wales. He was also responsible for pressure further north from the castle at Oswestry. William I was probably responsible for building Cardiff Castle when he visited Wales in 1081.

The Welsh, however, benefited not only from their terrain, much of which offered little advantage to the feudal cavalry of the Normans, but also from the military skills and determination honed by conflict within their own ranks, conflict that continued throughout the period, and was particularly acute in the 1070s and 1080s. The numerous Norman castles, both motte and bailey (earth and timber) and stone, provided refuge from Welsh attack, but could also be easily bypassed. Thus, fortress construction did not really stabilise Norman control. Instead, the Normans had to rely on light forces of their own to pursue Welsh raiders. Lightly armed cavalrymen, linked to castles, was one remedy used in Shropshire in the twelfth century. The employment of Welsh troops raised in the Marches was also important.

As in Cumbria under William II (1087–1100), the Normans in Wales sought to anchor their advance with castles and settlements, but the latter were restricted to lowland areas, especially in coastal south Wales. Nevertheless, Norman victories, such as the defeat and killing of Rhys ap Tewdwr, ruler of Deheubarth in 1093, were followed up by the seizure of territory by the land-hungry Norman baronage. Earlier, Hugh of Avranches, 'Hugh the Fat', Earl of Chester had pushed his way along the coast of north Wales. In 1088, he built a castle at Aberlleiniog on the east coast of Anglesey near Penmon. He also built castles at Bangor and Caernarfon. Norman pressure in north Wales was facilitated by civil war in Gwynedd.

The 'March' created by such gains was the result of Norman invasion and conquest, but it remained part of Wales, not a kind of no-man's-land between Wales and England. Marcher lordship has been seen as essentially Welsh political authority exercised by Anglo-Norman lords by right of conquest, Welsh royal rights in baronial hands. More recently, it has been presented as compact feudal lordships, with much in common with lordships in northern France (whose lords made war and peace and exercised 'high justice'), and with the 'castleries' of early Norman England. Marcher lordships came to look increasingly odd as the March stayed outside the orbit of the developing common law and centralised government in England, but that was not the case in the eleventh century. They introduced feudal land tenure and government to Wales. Feudalism rested on agricultural service by serfs. The existence of the unfree was not new, but it was now different because of the benefit to non-Welsh lords. The replacement of the open court-houses of Welsh rulers by castles was symptomatic of a major change of attitude. Nevertheless, much of the Marcher lordships was little altered: what was generally termed the 'Welshry' was held as before, now simply paying tribute to the new lords. The latter, however, more directly controlled the key positions; castles, boroughs where trade was permitted, and the manors on better land. The 'Welshry' was largely a matter of less attractive land.

The independence of the early Marchers was affected by the strong court connections and major landholdings in England and Normandy of many of their leading figures. Events in the March were always closely connected with wider politics. The Norman rulers were more concerned first with rebellion within England and secondly with conflict with France. Thus, the troubles in Wales at the beginning of the reign of Henry I (1100–35) were a sub-plot to the high political struggle between Henry and his elder brother Robert, Duke of Normandy. Another Robert, Robert of Bellême, the Montgomery Earl of Shrewsbury, who had lands from mid-Wales to Maine and whose power was broken by Henry in 1102, was not merely a disobedient Marcher baron but a supporter of Robert of Normandy. And although the Marcher lordships were part of Wales rather than England, they came to be regarded as held of the English Crown, which exercised rights of wardship, marriage and escheat over feudal vassals. Indeed, in the twelfth and thirteenth centuries, many lordships spent lengthy periods in the king's hands, or were pushed toward his supporters through marriage to heiresses.

The fighting was not all one way: the Welsh were able to regain the initiative, as in 1094, again during the English civil war in Stephen's reign (1135–54), and also in the mid-thirteenth century. In these periods much territory was regained. In 1094 much of Dyfed was reconquered and the Normans were pushed back from Ceredigion (Cardigan) and much of Dyfed, which the Earl of Shrewsbury had captured the previous year, and from west of the river Conwy. William II (1087–1100) failed to repair the situation in 1097. The following year, the Earl of Shrewsbury was killed in a naval battle with the Norse in the Menai Straits. Rhys ap Tewdwr's son Gruffydd (d. 1137) was able in the 1110s to inflict much damage on the Flemings newly settled in southern Wales by Henry I, and he also succeeded in capturing some castles. Nevertheless, he made little impact during the reign of Henry I (1100–35), a period of vigorous Anglo-Norman advance. The able and determined Henry, who sought to strengthen royal control over the Marchers, acquired the site of Carmarthen in 1109. At the lowest bridging point on the Tywi, Carmarthen became the major royal centre in south Wales. Henry developed it as a royal lordship with a castle and a royal borough. Kidwelly, Gower and Cemas were also organised as lordships. Pembroke had been founded as one under William II, and Henry I took control of it.

Henry was aided by the willingness of Welsh kings to seek his support. Similarly, the Welsh were willing to ally with the Norman lords. Thus Cadwgan, who played a major role in the 1094 rising, became the man of Robert, Earl of Shrewsbury in 1100, and accepted that he held Ceredigion as a fief from him. Cadwgan's son Owain, who abducted the wife of Gerald of Windsor, Constable of Pembroke, in 1109, was less accommodating, and Henry granted Ceredigion to Gilbert of Clare. He conquered it in 1111, and consolidated his position by building a number of castles. In 1114 and 1121, Henry invaded north Wales in person, receiving the submission of its rulers.

In addition, the authority of Canterbury was extended over the sees of St David's and Llandaff. Roman usage had spread in the Welsh Church prior to the Norman Conquest, replacing Celtic practices, Bangor in 768 being the first to conform, with St David's following by 928. This shift had no direct political consequences, although it increased links between Wales and the non-Celtic world. As in England, the role of clerical marriage and dynasties remained important until after the Conquest. It was then that Gregorian rules on the conduct of clerics, a diocesan and parochial structure and clear boundaries were introduced: Llandaff was established as a bishopric in 1107, St David's in 1115, Bangor in 1120, and St Asaph in 1143. The Normans sought to use the Church in order to weaken Welsh autonomy. Norman bishops were appointed at St David's in 1115 and at Llandaff in 1116. The claims of the see of St David's to metropolitan status and the headship of an independent Welsh Church were thwarted, not least by a careful selection of bishops, as with the thwarting of the independent-minded Gerald of Wales when he sought the see in 1176 and 1198–1203.

There was also a change in the monastic geography of Wales. Many Welsh foundations had their lands seized. The Normans initially established Benedectine priories, as at Monmouth and Abergavenny, followed by Cluniacs, as at Malpas, St Clears and Haverford. As in England, the Cistercian monastic order brought new energy in the mid-twelfth century. Cistercian abbeys were founded both by Norman – Tintern by Walter fitz Richard of Clare, Lord of Chepstow (1131), and Margam by Earl Robert of Gloucester (1147) – and by Welsh lords: Whitland (1140), Strata Florida (1164). Neath, founded in 1130, was a daughter house of Savigny and did not become a Cistercian house until 1147. Other Cistercian houses followed in the last quarter of the century. Llantarnam, founded in 1179, and Aberconwy (1186) were daughters of Strata Florida, Valle Crucis (1201) daughter of Strata Marcella (1170), itself a daughter of Whitland, as was Cwmhir which was the mother house of Cymer (1199). Valle Crucis was founded by the local ruler Madog ap Gruffydd Maelor, Strata Marcella by another, Owain Cyfeiliog, and Cymer was well endowed by Llywelyn the Great of Gwynedd. Thus, the Cistercian houses spread from south to central and then to north Wales, where the earlier monastic tradition was not in a good way. Whitland and Strata Florida, the latter eventually under the patronage of Rhys of Deheubarth, were the crucial intermediaries within native Wales. The monasteries played a major role in the development of sheep farming. They created large estates that proved the basis for long-distance trade. This helped to bring wealth to upland areas although much of it was to the benefit of the monasteries, leading, for example, to some impressive architecture.

Nevertheless, the Anglo-Norman achievement remained dependent on the calibre and interest of the monarch. The situation left by Henry I – conquest in the south and hegemony in the north – was reversed in 1136 at the outset of Stephen's reign: the Anglo-Normans were defeated in Cardigan and Gower. This was a period of civil war in England. Carmarthen fell in

1146, Tenby in 1153. The Welsh also drove back the Normans in north Wales. Had they been united, then the Welsh would have achieved even more. Even so, Gwynedd, Powys and Deheubarth were now free of immediate Norman pressure.

After the civil war and anarchy of Stephen's reign, Henry II (1154–89) sought to regain his grandfather's authority, but in Wales he had a formidable opponent in Gruffydd's son, Rhys (d. 1197) who revived the principality of Deheubarth, bringing it all under his control by 1155. Henry's fleet attacked Anglesey in 1157, sacking many churches, but the invaders were probably beaten at Tal Moelfre on the Menai Straits opposite Caernarfon. Henry II's invasion in 1158 led to the submission of several Welsh princes, but Rhys, angered by the extension of Anglo-Norman territorial claims, especially by Roger of Clare in Cardigan, attacked with success. Henry II again marched into Wales, forcing Rhys to submit in 1163, but he started fighting again in 1164, while Henry's invasion of Powys in 1165 was unsuccessful, in part because of heavy rainstorms. Rhys captured Cardigan in 1165. He really was the cause of Henry's campaign, but Owain of Gwynedd also led resistance. In 1167, in co-operation with Rhys, he took Rhuddlan, after a siege of three months. Rhys was a master of short-term submission, as well as of guerrilla warfare. He had learned how best to combat Norman cavalry. He also knew how to take advantage of fortress technology, improving Norman castles that he captured at Cardigan and Llandovery.

Henry accepted Rhys' position in 1171. Henry realised after the failure of his great 1164–5 campaign that a working relationship was the only answer. He also had commitments and problems in France. For the rest of Henry's reign, Rhys was in effect a powerful and independent sub-king, who, in return for doing homage, had effective control over his dominions, control that he strengthened by building his own castle. He endowed the new monastery at Strata Florida and patronised bards (poets) and harpists. As well as being Lord of Deheubarth, Rhys was 'Lord Rhys', Henry's Justiciar for south Wales; he may be compared with the other great feudatories of Henry II's empire. The lesser Welsh rulers of south Wales and northern Glamorgan were put under Rhys' protection. From his courts at Cardigan and Dinefwr, in the valley of the Tywi, Rhys dominated Wales and ensured stability. He was helped by divisions over the succession in Gwynedd after the death of Owain 'the Great' in 1170. These led to conflict in 1170 – the battle of Pentraeth, and again in 1194: the battles of

Porthaethwy and Coedanau. In 1194, the future Llywelyn the Great defeated his uncle Dafydd ab Owain, ruler of eastern Gwynedd.

When Henry died in 1189, Rhys took the initiative and the Welsh definitely had the advantage in the 1190s. The lordships of Cemaes and Kidwelly were captured. In 1196, Carmarthen, which had so often defied them, was taken by Rhys. Conflict was central to Welsh history in this period; the assessment of the impact of this incessant conflict is, however, difficult. Warfare could be devastating, but was less 'total' than modern warfare. The damage wrought by burning farmsteads and seizing animals was serious but less crippling to the economy in the long term than the devastation caused by the destruction of industrial plant. In *some* respects, a military campaign was similar in its impact to a very bad harvest. Many campaigns were in the nature of raids with the armies involved being small, yet the psychological effect of such warfare was probably considerable. It sustained a culture in which physical prowess and military leadership were important, but the warfare wrought damage in Wales rather than at a distance, as with the contemporary Crusades. Furthermore, much of this warfare was against other Welsh people, in some cases as auxiliaries of the rulers of

England. This was the bitter counterpart of talk of Welshness, although the same was true in France and Germany.

This was the period in which Gerald of Wales (*c.* 1146–1223), the Norman-Welsh Archdeacon of Brecon, was writing. Gerald was an educated cleric, only one quarter native Welsh, writing in the revived ethnographic tradition of what has been called the twelfth-century renaissance. His preaching tour of 1188 with Archbishop Baldwin, to gain support for the Third Crusade, was described in *Itinerarium Kambriae* (*The Journey Through Wales*) and he also wrote a *Descriptio Kambriae* (*Description of Wales*). Gerald is not that reliable a source, as when he denied that the Welsh built castles, and, as in other such works, there were numerous generalisations: 'the Welsh are the most particular in shaving the lower parts of the body . . . the Welsh sing their traditional songs, not in unison . . . but in parts, in many modes and modulations . . . Both sexes take great care of their teeth . . . for the Welsh generosity and hospitality are the greatest of all virtues'.

Nevertheless, these remarks were not necessarily inaccurate. Gerald had a clear sense of Welshness: he did not write of Gwynedd and Deheubarth as if their people were different. This reflected the idea of the Welsh as *cymry*, 'compatriots', a community united by shared and mutually-supporting culture, mythology, language, customs and laws. Despite their fissiparous politics, the Welsh saw themselves as one people occupying one country. However, the fragmentation of power and the practice of partible inheritance were, as Gerald argued, fundamental weaknesses in a political structure confronted with a powerful external threat. Rhys' quarrelome sons divided his kingdom. Again, however, this was scarcely unique to Wales. Division among heirs had destroyed the empire created by Charlemagne. Closer to home, William I had given Normandy to his eldest son, Robert, and England to his second, William II.

The problems of travelling round Wales was another cause of division. The terrain was frequently difficult, not only the mountains but also the many rivers and estuaries that had to be crossed. River fords were affected by seasonal spates, and estuary crossings by tides or, as with the Neath, quicksands. Travel overland was not helped by the poor quality of the roads and tracks. The Roman roads were not in a good state of repair, and there had been no system of construction since. Bandits exacerbated the situation, and were a particular problem in the extensive woodlands of Wales. Wolves were also a hazard.

Cymru was taken closest to political fulfilment by Llywelyn the Great (d. 1240), grandson of Owain the Great, and by his grandson, Llywelyn ap Gruffydd, 'the Last' (d. 1282) of Gwynedd, uniting native Wales (*pura Wallia*). Gwynedd was the part of Wales without Norman settlement and the area most remote from Norman power. Its mountains were also a formidable military obstacle, and it was difficult for any invasion force to find supplies locally. The importance of Gwynedd was accentuated by the problems of Deheubarth and Powys both of which were divided, the first, after the death of Rhys in 1197, because of disputes between his sons and the second because of a permanent division between two branches of the dynasty after 1166.

The thirteenth century is the period when Gwynedd finally emerged as the dominant power and when the two Llywelyns sought to create a Welsh political unit and single political authority where none had existed before. It is not known who thought of this in the first place, but the new development was associated with the general growth of jurisdictional definition and written government in the thirteenth century, together with the growth in moveable wealth, which gave a sharper focus to princely claims everywhere. In Wales, traditions of 'national' history and identity, which had been invented and propagated by the native intelligentsia, were given more political reality by 'modernising' princes, who built castles, developed rights and resources, founded monasteries and granted borough charters, and were served by a small circle of administrators (including churchmen educated outside Wales). In order to resist English claims, the princes had to copy English developments, administration and political aspirations. This was part of a process of administrative consolidation that was common throughout western Europe. It was not necessarily state-building, for this process also took place within major aristocratic fiefdoms. To a certain extent, Scotland experienced the same process as Gwynedd, and the dynasty there was helped by its royal status and by the succession of three able rulers, William the Lion (1165–1214), Alexander II (1214–49) and Alexander III (1249–86), who defeated foreign invasion and overcame domestic opponents. Furthermore, whereas the Kings of Scotland had welcomed Anglo-Norman barons, granting them land, and used their energy and skills to strengthen the Scottish state, no such synergy occurred in Wales, certainly not in *pura Wallia*. This was a major weakness that reflected in large part a lack of opportunity. The Anglo-Norman attitude in Wales was expropriatory and there was not the land to spare. Yet, the failure to ensure long-term co-operation across the cultural divide was not only to lead to weakness, but also to lack of recognition. In Wales, the object of the two Llywelyns was to extend overlordship over the other native rulers and at the same time to persuade the English crown to accept the homage of the prince of Gwynedd for the whole of native Wales, the other rulers having done homage to the prince. What was needed to confirm this was a treaty with the crown.

The princes of Gwynedd also built stone castles, including at Dolwyddelan, Dolbadarn and Criccieth. These were different from earlier earth and wooden structures, such as Dafydd ab Owain's castle at Rhuddlan, not only because they were stronger militarily – they did not burn – but also because they were an assertion of strength. The castles were designed to protect routes through Gwynedd. The size of their garrisons is unclear, but they represented an immediately available force. Compared to the castles built later by Edward I, the Welsh castles had simple plans, but they were an advance on what had come earlier. Dolbadarn's round keep was a strong feature and Criccieth's twin-towered gatehouse was state-of-the-art. Similarly, the princes of Powys had built Castell Coch – the Red Castle, now Powys Castle. This was captured by the English under Hubert Walter in 1196, but regained the following year by the dynamic Prince of southern Powys (Powys Wenwynwyn), Gwenwynwyn ab Owain.

Llywelyn the Great first established himself by beating his uncles (1194–1202), and in 1208, as an ally of King John of England, he conquered southern Powys from Gwenwynwyn, who was an arch rival of his kinsman Llywelyn. Gwenwynwyn had fallen out with John and was detained by him. Llywelyn followed this up by seizing Ceredigion (Cardiganshire), but in 1208 he in turn fell out with John who restored Gwenwynwyn. Like his father, Henry II, John considered it appropriate and necessary to intervene in north Wales. Supported by Powys and the sons of Rhys, John campaigned in Gwynedd, driving Llywelyn back into Snowdonia and destroying Bangor Cathedral. Welsh assistance to John paralleled the support Edwards I, II and III were to find in Scotland a century later, although in Wales there was far less sense of a political unit. Llywelyn was forced to sue for peace and to cede north-east Wales, but, in 1212, he rose again, this time supported by the other major Welsh princes. Llywelyn allied with Philip Augustus of France, an alliance probably engineered by Pope Innocent III, another of John's opponents. The English lost their new castles in Gwynedd, and John was also handicapped by serious opposition to his policies in England. He was obliged in Magna Carta (1215) to promise to restore all lands illegally taken from Welshmen. Much of south Wales then rose with Llywelyn's assistance and he was able to raze Carmarthen castle to the ground. In 1216, at a sort of parliament or council meeting of Welsh rulers at Aberdyfi, Llywelyn dealt with competing territorial claims within *pura Wallia*. Llywelyn alone used the title of Prince, and he sought to act as the legal overlord of the other Welsh rulers. This was designed to lessen the chance of the king of England meddling in Welsh politics. Borrowing English royal techniques, Llywelyn used 'great' and 'privy' seals.

Llywelyn did homage to John's infant son Henry III (1216–72) after the Peace of Worcester in 1218, although maintaining his position against both English and Welsh rivals, having in 1216 invaded Powys, forcing Gwenwynwyn to flee to England where he died. His line was not restored to Powys until Llywelyn's death in 1240. In 1219, Llywelyn devastated Pembrokeshire and, in 1221, defeated Rhys Gryg of Deheubarth who had joined William Marshal, 2nd Earl of Pembroke. Llywelyn annexed Kidwelly and Gower in 1221, but his siege of Builth Castle the following year was unsuccessful, and in 1223 William Marshal returned from Ireland and drove Llywelyn from many of his recent gains, including

Carmarthen. Llywelyn benefited from the support of a number of prominent Marcher and Norman-Irish barons. In 1226, Llywelyn and William Marshal made a peace.

Llywelyn attacked again in 1228, unsuccessfully besieging Montgomery Castle. When Henry III advanced, Llywelyn made peace and renewed his homage, but hostilities flared up anew in 1231 when Llywelyn captured Montgomery and Usk and invaded Gwent in south-east Wales, a region that had for long been under secure Anglo-Norman control. The town of Caerleon was burnt down, but the castle successfully resisted. Neath and Kidwelly, however, were captured. In 1233, he took advantage of the rebellion of Richard Marshal, 3rd Earl of Pembroke, to ally with him and campaign together successfully in Gwent. Llywelyn's siege of Carmarthen Castle was unsuccessful, however, and Llywelyn agreed to a truce in 1234, while his ally was killed in Ireland. He had not retained control of Gower or Kidwelly, but both Builth and Cardigan were recognised as under him.

The willingness of Marcher barons to ally with Llywelyn underlines the danger of seeing politics or warfare in simple terms of Welsh versus English. Llywelyn married his daughters into Marcher families, with important political implications. Nevertheless, allowing for the limited validity of the Welsh/English contrast, his reign saw an important shift of the balance of advantage towards the Welsh. One testimony was the extensive improvements to fortifications, for example those made by the Marshal family at Chepstow, Cilgerran, Pembroke and Usk, by the crown at Montgomery, and by others at Bronllys, Skenfrith and Tretower. The location of these works was a testimony to the range of Welsh power.

Llywelyn died in 1240, still in control of native Wales, among the Cistercians of Aberconwy whom he had actively supported. He was also a generous patron of the native bards who celebrated his talents. Llywelyn helped unify the laws and encouraged a sense of unity. Nevertheless, he had failed to secure the treaty with the English crown necessary to cement his position: Llywelyn sought recognition and an assured succession. The principality he had built up depended entirely on his personality and had little institutional framework to sustain it, so it fell apart on his death. As such, Gwynedd was different to England or Scotland. As in other monarchical states, however, stability was threatened by the succession.

Llywelyn sought to leave a clear succession by designating Dafydd, his son by John's illegitimate daughter Joan, and gathering all the princes of Wales together to swear fealty in 1238, but this was contested by Llywelyn's eldest son Gruffydd, the child of an irregular union, although possibly not so in Welsh terms. Dafydd may have been the chosen successor because his mother was a Plantagenet which could help to admit him to the contemporary European royal network and thus bring a measure of international recognition. Llywelyn also recognised the problems created by the established practice of equal division among heirs.

In 1239, Gruffydd was seized by Dafydd at a peace conference and imprisoned. Gruffydd, however, enjoyed considerable support, while Dafydd suffered from a hostile turn of events, helping create the impression that he lacked his father's ability and personality. In 1241, Henry III forced Dafydd to hand Gruffydd over to his custody, providing a means of putting pressure on Dafydd. In 1244, Dafydd made an abortive bid to become a papal vassal, while Gruffydd tried to escape from the Tower of London using a rope made from his linen. However, he was heavy and broke his neck. War then resumed between Dafydd and the English Marcher lords. He invaded Herefordshire in 1244 and captured Mold in 1245. Henry III advanced with a great army to Deganwy in Gwynedd, but Dafydd retired into Snowdonia and, short of supplies, Henry had to retreat, although much damage was done by ruthless devastation. An English fleet from Ireland meanwhile attacked Anglesey.

However, the nature of the succession and the practice of partible inheritance again weakened Gwynedd. Dafydd died childless in 1246, and Gruffydd's eldest sons Owain and Llywelyn divided the inheritance, performing homage to Henry III in 1247 after the English seneschal of Carmarthen had overrun the southern dependencies of Gwynedd. In addition, by the Treaty of Woodstock of 1247, all the lands east of the Conwy went to Henry, a major extension of royal power. The hegemony that Llywelyn had built up within Wales collapsed. The rulers of Powys and Deheubarth now gave allegiance to Henry III, while the Treaty of Woodstock established the terms of that from the rulers of Gwynedd.

As so often, the princes of Gwynedd now fought each other, Owain, supported by his younger brother Dafydd, attacking Llywelyn in 1254. Their clash was over the share of lands for Dafydd, and to resolve the problem of there being two rival princes. The victorious Llywelyn gained sole power in Gwynedd in 1255, imprisoned Owain and set out to restore the dominions of his grandfather. This led to tension with the Welsh leaders in south Wales, who did not wish to be ruled by Gwynedd. Furthermore, in 1254 Henry granted his eldest son Edward, a dynamic prince, the Earldom of Chester and the royal lands in Wales. This led to a new energy in the enforcement of the pretensions of the English crown. As Earl of Chester, Edward was a key figure to the east of Gwynedd, but insensitive rule by his officials caused trouble. In south-west Wales, Edward's agents sought, unsuccessfully, to establish a shire system using English laws. In contrast, the cantons of contemporary Switzerland had a much easier evolution in their quest for autonomy and then independence as Habsburg rulers became more interested in Austria from the 1270s.

Llywelyn sought to stop Edward's plans, overrunning north-east Wales in 1256 and central Wales in 1256–7, and invading south Wales in 1257. Gruffydd ap Gwenwynwyn of Powys refused to acknowledge Llywelyn as overlord and in 1257 fled to England. Henry III's advance in 1257 achieved nothing and Llywelyn continued to extend his power, now at the expense of the Marcher lords, taking Builth Castle in 1260 and Brecon in 1262. Enjoying support throughout unconquered Wales, Llywelyn backed Simon de Montfort and his baronial allies against Henry III, and in 1263 the leading castle in north Wales, Deganwy, was surrendered by its blockaded garrison. The same year, Gruffydd of Powys submitted to Llywelyn because of pressure on him by his Marcher neighbours. In 1264, de Montfort defeated Henry at Lewes. In 1265,

Henry, held since Lewes by de Montfort, was made to sign the Pipton treaty granting Llywelyn the 'Principality', with the homage of all the Welsh magnates, as well as Hawarden and Montgomery. De Montfort was defeated at Evesham but, by the Treaty of Montgomery (1267), as part of the post-war reconciliation, Henry felt it prudent to grant Llywelyn essentially the same terms that had been agreed in 1265. The concession of Llywelyn's newly-claimed title of Prince of Wales, a title earlier used by Owain of Gwynedd, Rhys ap Gruffydd and Dafydd, indicated the extent to which the reimposition of royal power in England after the defeat of de Montfort did not extend to Wales. This was the treaty with the English crown that Llywelyn the Great had not achieved.

Between 1272 and 1277, however, there was a sequence of crises in Anglo-Welsh relations, although it is unlikely that either side wanted war. Llywelyn failed to do homage to Edward I, who came to the throne in 1272. Llywelyn lacked the ability to define a compromise such as his grandfather and Rhys of Deheubarth had reached, and the limited resources of his principality made it difficult to pay Edward. Llywelyn's repeated refusal of homage was a serious provocation. In 1274, Llywelyn's brother and heir, Dafydd, who held Gwynedd east of the Conwy, and Gruffydd of Powys plotted to assassinate Llywelyn, but were detected. Gruffydd fled to England and Llywelyn took Pool (Powis) Castle.

In 1277, Edward set out to settle relations. He invaded with massive force and the support of the other Welsh rulers and the Welsh exiles. While secondary forces advanced in central and south Wales, the former accompanied by Gruffydd of Powys, Edward attacked Gwynedd, using his navy to cut off Anglesey, Gwynedd's major source of food, a policy Gerald of Wales had earlier advised. Bottling up Llywelyn in Snowdonia, Edward kept him short of supplies until, on 9 November, Llywelyn surrendered. He accepted Edward's terms at the Treaty of Aberconwy (1277).

Llywelyn was made to do homage to Edward and to surrender the lands east of the Conwy. His Welsh opponents were granted territories, and the homage of most of the Welsh leaders was transferred to the king: Welsh Wales was not to be united by Gwynedd. The Principality was now restricted to Snowdonia and Anglesey. Edward anchored his position with a major programme of fortification at Aberystwyth, Builth, Flint, Rhuddlan and Ruthin.

The peace was followed by an Anglicisation of government and Church that created problems. Archbishop

Peckham of Canterbury told Llywelyn that Welsh customs were only to be observed if reasonable. English rule in north-east Wales was unpopular: timber, common and judicial rights were abused. A conflict of laws led to the outbreak of a new war. Emphasising the law of Wales, Dafydd rebelled in 1282 and won the support of his brother, himself angered by his treatment by Edward, although it is not really known when Llywelyn actually joined the 1282 war: possibly in June, after the death of his wife while giving birth to a daughter.

The war began in March 1282. Dafydd attacked the other native Welsh rulers and seized the royal castles of Flint and Rhuddlan and the new Marcher castle at Hawarden. There was also rebellion in west Wales and the valley of the Tywi. Edward saw this as a treasonable rebellion and repeated his strategy of 1277, although his attempt to support his attack on Gwynedd by an invasion from Anglesey failed in November, when a bridge of boats collapsed and the attacking force was defeated. Llywelyn, fearing winter starvation, broke out of Snowdonia and was killed in a skirmish at the Irfon Bridge near Builth on 11 December. His head was taken to London for display. Dafydd, who was largely responsible for the rebellion, became a fugitive in Snowdonia. In 1283, he was captured by hostile Welsh and executed at Shrewsbury by first being hanged, then having his entrails torn from his body, which was then beheaded and quartered: the fate of a traitor. That year, Edward overran all of Gwynedd, taking such positions as Criccieth Castle. In the event, the castles the Welsh built did not delay or deter Edward's armies to any real extent. The sole significant siege of a Welsh castle was Dryslwyn in 1287, during a rebellion in south Wales. They were places of last retreat, and did not play a significant strategic role.

The contrasting military fates of Wales and Scotland cannot be attributed to divisions among the Welsh and the extent to which the English received Welsh support; the same was true of Scotland. The failures of earlier expeditions indicated that there was no inevitability in Welsh defeat, but the English were helped by the relatively compact nature of Gwynedd and its relatively low population, by the proximity of English bases, especially Chester and Shrewsbury, by their far superior resources in terms of men, money and supplies, by naval power and by the absence of foreign assistance for Llywelyn: there was no help from France or Scotland and the only intervention from Ireland was of troops sent to help the English. The fate of Scotland on the other hand was to be greatly affected by English commitments in France, both in the 1290s and in the fourteenth century.

Llywelyn was no more powerful in terms of financial resources than a middle-ranking English earl. The disparity between English and Welsh resources was immense, and Edward was far better at mobilising his resources than Henry III had been. Feats such as the 1282 pontoon bridge across the Menai Straits illustrate this.

There was little fighting in the form of battles, but Edward was able to grind the Welsh down by continuing his campaign – or at least staying in Wales – right through the winter of 1282–3, and did much the same in 1294–5 when the Welsh rebelled. In part, Edward just about starved the Welsh into surrender. The English were also fortunate in being able to draw the Welsh into battle in 1282 (Llywelyn's defeat and death at Irfon Bridge) and 1295 (defeat of Madog at Maes Moydog).

Antagonism to Llywelyn, even from within his own family, was also important. The wars could almost be described as civil wars: certainly more Welshmen fought for Edward I than against him, prefiguring the situation in Scotland when the Duke of Cumberland defeated the Jacobites at Culloden in 1746. Edward was able to recruit on a very large scale in south Wales. The destruction of the line of Gwynedd and part of the Welsh ruling class ensured that Edward's conquest was much more solid than earlier English successes in Wales.

TWO

FROM CONQUEST TO THE SEVENTEENTH CENTURY

POST-CONQUEST WALES

The conquest was secured by a new military order and followed by a governmental settlement. The English presence in Wales had for long been based on castles, and the campaigns of 1277 and 1282 were each followed by extensive construction. After 1277, there was work at Aberystwyth, Builth, Flint and Rhuddlan, but after 1282 there were new sites for fortification and a new strategic task because Gwynedd was now crown property. The major new fortresses designed by James of St George – Caernarfon, a fortress-palace, the intended centre of royal power, Conwy, Harlech and Beaumaris – were all coastal castles that could be supplied by sea. Most of the heavy building materials for their construction were brought the same way. The construction of these massive stone-built works was a formidable undertaking, costing at least £93,000 and using thousands of conscripted English workers. Marcher castles were also constructed at Chirk, Denbigh and Holt, and, further

afield, castles at Llawhaden and Kidwelly were strengthened. In the thirteenth century, native Welsh rulers had
built castles, such as Dolbadarn and Castell y Bere, but
now castle-building was to be under English control only.
The Welsh castles at Criccieth and Dolwyddelan, as well
as Castell y Bere, were taken over and strengthened.
Edward's power also enabled him to order that
undergrowth within 200 feet of main roads be removed
in order to lessen the risk of ambush.

The crucial element of the new political settlement was
the end of the de facto independent Welsh principality.
The politico-constitutional achievements of the rulers of
Gwynedd were to serve as a basis for later rule by Edward
I and his successors. The principality recognised in 1267
did survive. It formed a dependency of England from
1284, not represented in Parliament or under the English
courts, and was granted in 1301 to Edward I's eldest son,
the future Edward II, who was created Prince of Wales
and who had been born in Caernarfon Castle in 1285.
The principality would not be annexed to England until
1536 – but it was no longer independent. It was, instead,
allocated an essentially honorific, rather than independent, position for the heirs to the English throne.

Applying feudal law, Edward I saw himself as the heir
to Llywelyn's forfeited estate and the crown thus

obtained much of Wales, including all of Gwynedd. Signs of independence were carefully suppressed. Llywelyn's seals were melted, his silver made into plate, and his princely coronet displayed in Westminster Abbey. Owain ap Gruffydd ap Gwenwynwyn, the last hereditary Prince of Upper Powys, renounced his princely title in 1286, the year in which he succeeded his father Gruffydd, and paid homage to Edward I as Baron de la Pole (i.e. of Pool or Powis Castle). Edward sought to eliminate the Gwynedd dynasty by putting the daughters of Llywelyn and Dafydd into convents in Lincolnshire and by imprisoning the sons of Dafydd in Bristol.

In effect the 'frontier' had been closed and it was therefore necessary and possible to create a new administrative and judicial structure for the crown lands. The Statute of Wales issued at Rhuddlan on 3 March 1284 extended the English shrieval system to Anglesey, Caernarvon, Flint and Merioneth, in addition to Cardigan and Carmarthen which had emerged as counties earlier in the thirteenth century. English criminal law was introduced, although civil law remained largely Welsh. The extension of the shrieval system involved a considerable redrawing of borders. Existing local government units were reshaped and, in the case of the *cantref* of Dunoding, divided between Caernarvon and Merioneth, ceased to exist. The introduction of English criminal law led to a new office, that of sheriff, to take charge of law and order and justice in the county. In the long term, this lessened the role and relevance of the clans, a major social change that was to help prepare the way for new patterns of identity and obedience. The sheriff presided over the county court, as a new institution, and the courts also dealt with a range of administrative taxes, such as the granting of brewing licences.

Caernarfon and Carmarthen became centres of royal administration, while the new castles of Aberystwyth, Beaumaris, Caernarfon, Conwy, Denbigh, Flint and Rhuddlan were associated with new or transformed towns that were created for settlement by English craftsmen and merchants and that were clearly seen as centres of English influence and culture, although by 1305 the richest burgess in Beaumaris was a Welshman. These towns were given privileges in order to ensure their success and to focus trade and wealth on them. The privileges included a certain amount of immunity from royal officials in town government, the right to hold markets and fairs, and exemption from particular tolls. The towns were also adjuncts to the castles. They were protected by walls and were part of the same defensive position. The Cistercian abbey of Aberconwy, where

Llywelyn the Great was buried, was re-sited at Maenan, up the valley of the Conwy, in order to clear the site for the castle and town Edward I founded at Conwy to protect the coastal route from Chester to Gwynedd.

The conquest of Gwynedd was a major achievement for Edward I, although the conscious imitation of the Theodosian land wall of Constantinople with its polychrome stonework at Caernarfon was a disproportionate echo of imperial power. The eagle-crowned turrets of Caernarfon were probably designed to strike an echo with the Welsh tradition about Maximus.

Although Cornwall was the first 'frontier' to be closed, it had never posed a military challenge comparable to Gwynedd, let alone Wales. Edward's conquest moved the zone of military power forward. It made larger defensive works in Cheshire and Shropshire relatively valueless and the castles there fell into ruin. The very failures of Edward's father and grandfather (Henry III and John) had encouraged him to act, as did the extent to which the Welsh problem was not separate from English domestic politics: indeed Llywelyn had married a daughter of Simon de Montfort, much to the anger of Edward.

There was further resistance after 1283, including a revolt in 1287. This was not a major national rising; it was limited to Carmarthenshire and led by one of the

Welsh lords who had supported Edward in 1282 and who was disappointed with his reward. The heavy taxation levied in 1292–3 to support Edward I's projected expedition to France, however, led to discontent in England and a serious rebellion in Wales in 1294–5 led by Madog, a member of a cadet branch of the Gwynedd dynasty. It was primarily a protest against government policy rather than English control. For example, the harsh Sheriff of Anglesey, Roger de Pulesdon, was hanged at Caernarfon by an Anglesey official when the town and castle were captured.

The revolt broke out simultaneously in the north, the west and the south-east, which suggests concerted planning. The castle programme had not deterred rebellion. The uncompleted castle at Caernarfon was taken and the town walls destroyed, although the castle at Conwy successfully resisted attack. After the initial English response had had little success, Edward intervened. The Earl of Warwick defeated Madog in a night attack on his camp in 1295 and Edward received the submission of the Welsh. He then took steps to press on with his programme of fortification. Caernarfon was recovered and completed. Beaumaris on Anglesey was begun in 1295 in response to Madog's rebellion. However, after two or three years in which much was constructed, Edward's attention focused on Scotland and Beaumaris was never completed. A classic concentric castle built to a very regular geometric plan, with massive gatehouses, it also had its own harbour.

Wales was affected by serious economic problems in the fourteenth century, an aspect of a more widespread demographic and economic crisis in western Europe, in part caused by population pressure on limited food resources. There are indications that the population fell, helping to reduce pressure. This, for example, was seen in Penllyn between 1293 and 1318 where a large fall in population led to adequate food resources being available.

It is unclear how far the Welsh saw themselves as a conquered people. There was resentment at the dominance of administration and Church by Englishmen, and also at the commercial privileges granted to the inhabitants of the new towns. The Welsh remained overwhelmingly rural as well as relatively poor compared to the population in England. The political, administrative and legal system worked to the benefit of the English, who had the necessary patrons at court, and this was crucial in the administration of justice. More generally, the Welsh had to pay both for the Principality and for the Marcher lordships, with judicial fees, fines and communal subsidies.

Edward tried to do something about Welsh grievances. In 1316, one Llywelyn Bren had been dismissed from his official position in Glamorgan by an English superior and, when he complained, was accused of sedition. Edward II rejected Llewelyn's attempt to justify himself, and this had led to Llewelyn's revolt, but his rising was suppressed by the overwhelming force of the Marcher lords.

Such an account can be seen as an indication of mistreatment, and yet it is also significant that Llywelyn, like many Welsh landholders, had held high office. In 1322, the Welsh Sheriff of Anglesey remained loyal to Edward II when his English counterparts in Caernarfon and Merioneth and John, Lord Charleton, a powerful Marcher baron, rebelled, a sign in part of the extent to which the latter were closely linked to English factional politics. Just as generations of Welsh princes, especially in Powys, had looked to the English for support, so others were able to accommodate themselves to the new regime. The conquest of Gwynedd was not followed by a wholesale expropriation of property comparable to that after the Norman conquest of England and, although the Church was brought more into line with English practice, there was again nothing to compare with the situation under William I. Edward I refounded Aberconwy Abbey:

he did not end it. At the local level, there was little change: the same families, the traditional leaders of the community, remained in charge.

Much of Wales, especially south Wales, was still under the control of the Anglo-Norman Marcher families that had conquered it. Known collectively as the Welsh March, these lordships were not integrated into shires and were autonomous: their lords had effective administrative and legal control. Prominent lordships included Glamorgan which belonged to the Clares, Maelienydd and Radnor (Mortimers), Brecon (Bohuns), Abergavenny (Hastings), Ruthin (Greys), and Pembroke (Valences). Edward I thus made no attempt to create an integrated state: instead, he dealt with the immediate problem of Gwynedd. Yet the great power of the Marcher lords was a potential threat to the stability of the crown, and Edward tried to assert his powers as sovereign over them too. While this contrast in government remained, royal authority was fragmented and there was no governmental agency that could lend bureaucratic shape to the notion of Wales. Most Marcher lordships gradually came, by marriage or inheritance, into the possession of magnate families. The Powys inheritance came to Owain ap Gruffydd's daughter Hawys in 1309. She married Sir John Charleton, and thus the former principality of Upper Powys became a Marcher lordship. In 1312, Charleton and his wife successfully defended Powis Castle against a rising by her uncle Gruffydd de la Pole, who wanted the inheritance himself. Their feud, frequently violent, continued until the 1330s and indicated the interaction of inheritance disputes, regional and national politics, and issues of Welshness. In 1316, Charleton helped raise troops to suppress the rising of Llywelyn Bren.

The Welsh played an important role in support of the English crown in the fourteenth century. John Charleton raised large forces to help Edward II in Scotland and took Welsh troops with him when he was appointed 'custos' of Ireland by Edward III in 1337. Many bowmen and spearmen from all over Wales, especially from Gwent, served in the Hundred Years War fought with France between 1337 and 1453. Scottish ships were a threat: the Scots raided Holyhead in 1315 and attacked Beaumaris in 1381. Between 1369 and 1378, Owain ap Thomas ap Rhodri or, as the French called him, Yvain de Galles, the great-nephew of Llywelyn ap Gruffydd and the last heir of the Gwynedd dynasty, was active in French service. In 1369 and 1372, there were abortive expeditions to Wales and he was assassinated by an English agent at Mortagne-sur-Gironde in 1378.

The rising of Owain Glyn Dŵr (Owen Glendower) in 1400–8 was an indication of the extent of disaffection and the survival of separatist feeling. Causes included the general tensions of the second half of the fourteenth century, disillusionment with the English crown on the part of the leaders of the native community, and the social and economic grievances which were subsumed by the revolt. Yet Glyn Dŵr's earlier career also testified to the process of accommodation. An important landowner at Glyndyfrdwy and Sycharth in Clwyd who was a descendant of Welsh ruling dynasties, he was also a squire to the Earl of Arundel. In 1385, he took part in Richard II's Scottish campaign. Glyn Dŵr's revolt had probably been planned for a long time and may be seen as part of a whole series of revolts which occurred in Europe between about 1350 and 1450. It was in some ways a reaction to the successive crises of the fourteenth century, including the plague outbreak known as the Black Death which had hit Wales hard in 1349–50 and then again in 1361 and 1369, but it was also a protest by the leaders of the native community at their being neglected by the authorities and at heavy taxation.

The removal of Richard II, who had enjoyed some popularity in Wales, by Henry Bolingbroke, who became Henry IV in 1399, helped disrupt patterns of authority, and also called into question the legitimacy of the regime. Furthermore, the wider legitimacy of 'foreign' rule was challenged by the prevalence, in vaticinatory poetry, of bardic myths that saw the Welsh as different and destined to regain Wales. Dissatisfaction within the Welsh Church with the positions held by English clerics was also important and led to opposition from Welsh clerics. The Abbots of Bardsey and Maenan had to seek Henry IV's peace in 1400. Lewis Byford, who became Bishop of Bangor in 1404, supported Glyn Dŵr.

Proclaiming himself 'Prince of Wales' in September 1400, Glyn Dŵr rose in north Wales, helped by dissatisfaction with the financial demands of English landowners and by kinship and marriage ties among the Welsh landowners. He first attacked Ruthin. Henry IV led an army into Wales in October 1400, but Glyn Dŵr avoided battle and in 1401 briefly seized Conwy Castle and invaded central Wales, although he was unsuccessful at Caernarfon in November 1401 and again in November 1403. Fresh victories against Marcher forces and unsuccessful, though destructive, advances by royal armies were followed by negotiations with English opponents of Henry and attempts to win Scottish, Irish and French support. In 1403, Glyn Dŵr allied with Henry Percy, 1st Earl of Northumberland, but the Percy forces under the Earl's son 'Hotspur', Sir Henry Percy, were defeated that year at the battle of Shrewsbury, and the Percy rebellion ended. Despite this major check, Glyn Dŵr pressed on. Carmarthen and most of south Wales were captured in 1403, Cardiff, Harlech and Aberystwyth in 1404. Glyn Dŵr sealed a treaty of alliance with the French who promised assistance, and sought to organise regular government, as well as an independent Church and universities. His seal showed Glyn Dŵr bearing princely regalia and enthroned. A Welsh Parliament was summoned at Machynlleth, with four representatives from each commote. This was an aspect of the process by which developments in Wales emulated those further afield. There were also plans to break ties between the Welsh Church and Canterbury, and to create two universities, one each for north and south Wales. Throughout the emphasis was on Wales, not on a part of it. Some of the English Marchers bought peace from Welsh raids by truces. In 1405, Glyn Dŵr agreed the Tripartite Indenture with Edmund Mortimer and Henry Percy, Earl of Northumberland, by which they were to depose Henry IV and divide England. Glyn Dŵr's share included, besides Wales, England west of a line from the Mersey to the source of the Trent and then to the Severn just north of Worcester. Mortimer, who married Glyn

Dŵr's daughter, was the uncle and namesake of the young Earl of March, who had a claim on the throne. The agreement was unrealistic, but it captured a central feature of the geopolitics of Welsh independence. In the face of English enmity, this was only going to be plausible if assistance and resources could be obtained from supporters outside Wales. Ireland was not an option, because the English were established in eastern Ireland. Indeed in 1405 an army from Dublin landed at Holyhead, defeated Glyn Dŵr's supporters at Rhos-meirch, ravaged Anglesey, and returned to Ireland with the coffin of St Cybi. However, in the 1400s the situation was far more promising as far as both France and domestic opposition within England were concerned. This was the chance for independence, but it proved impossible to combine forces effectively. Percy rebelled for a second time, only to be defeated again in 1405.

A French expeditionary force arrived in 1405 and Carmarthen fell for the second time, but, in the face of English naval power, the French faltered. In 1405, Glyn Dŵr, with French help, advanced as far as Worcester, but then withdrew. Although another of Henry IV's expeditions achieved very little, his vigorous son Prince 'Hal', later Henry V, began to inflict serious defeats. Anglesey submitted in November 1406. Harlech and Aberystwyth were recaptured in 1408, and the south was entirely reconquered. Percy rebelled for the third time, but was defeated and killed on Bramham Moor in 1408. Support for the rebellion ebbed, although it remained important in Gwynedd; and the English were increasingly successful.

Glyn Dŵr disappeared in 1415. He has served in the late twentieth century as a potent symbol of Welsh nationalism, and is certainly more appropriate for that than the princely house of Gwynedd, who spent much of their energy fighting each other and other Welsh rulers. There was, however, a strong opposition to him among some native gentry as well; they saw alliance with the Crown as the best way to maintain their privileges. Opposition to Glyn Dŵr was strongest in south and east Wales, in both of which there was long experience of English control and practices of co-operation that retained considerable vitality. Dafydd Gam, the possible origin of Shakespeare's character Fluellen, was loyal to Henry IV and was rewarded with confiscated lands. Glyn Dŵr was indeed abandoned by some prominent supporters: Gwilym ap Gruffydd of Penrhyn rallied to Henry IV in 1405 and was rewarded with many of the lands of the rebellious Tudors of Penmynydd.

Glyn Dŵr was a warrior of his times who used devastation without remorse. The cathedrals of St Asaph and Bangor were burnt down, as were Cardiff, Carmarthen, Nefyn and Pwlheli, but Prince Hal also brought widespread destruction, and the English had often used this technique. Glyn Dŵr used guerrilla tactics, including devastation – the destruction of homes and farm implements and the seizure of farm animals were for many, especially the weak, equivalent to sentences of death or at least severe hardship and malnutrition. These tactics did not challenge the English castle garrisons effectively. Heavily outnumbered, Glyn Dŵr prudently avoided battle on many occasions and his military career was not conventionally heroic. More significantly, he was leading his followers toward a dead end: English power was such that it was only possible during periods of English civil conflict, such as the Percy rising of 1403, for Welsh opponents to make much headway. At other times, the weight of English resources told. Had Glyn Dŵr been more successful, Wales would have been exposed to decades of incessant conflict and the Welsh to deep divisions. The energy and ability of Prince Henry ensured that this was a particularly bad moment to begin a struggle that would last many years. As with many leaders, Glyn Dŵr was more useful as a dead symbol for posterity.

The rising led to much distrust and was followed by the after-effects of economic disruption, as well as the collection of rent arrears, fines and banditry, but not by new governmental arrangements. The Marcher lords remained the crucial political figures; accordingly the Welsh were second-class subjects not, for example, sending representatives to Parliament. The penal laws of Henry IV forbade the Welsh to hold land in boroughs and also Welsh men to marry English women. In the new charter that Edward, Lord Charleton of Powys, gave Welshpool in 1406, great care was taken to keep the 'foreign Welsh' away. They had massacred the English citizens of Welshpool. However, Charleton also took care to obtain a royal pardon for his rebellious Welsh tenantry.

Still, from the fourteenth century, social changes were working towards the emergence of a Welsh gentry class. The Black Death was instrumental in breaking down the old landowning patterns, and this was further encouraged by the disruption of Glyn Dŵr's rising. Kindred patrimonies (*gwelyau*) and the shared status that was their central feature declined in favour of individual ownership. Inheritance and tenurial changes – especially the introduction of English forms of land tenure, the development of primogeniture and greater freedom in the disposal of land – facilitated the development of freehold estates and curbed the process of fragmentation among heirs. Landholders gained wealth through military or administrative service or marriage. They acquired crown lands, built substantial dwellings and developed political pretensions within the framework of an English-ruled and -governed Wales. Discrete estates were being built up and a body of gentry developing. The bards sustained a sense of Welsh identity, and were extensively patronised by the *uchelwyr* (literally 'the high men': gentry), although not in Anglicised colonised regions such as south Pembrokeshire and Gower, but those who were politically significant did not see this identity in terms of independence. As the kindred groupings broke up, patterns of identity altered although ties of lineage were still important as markers of status and a means of patronage. Royal authority had replaced that of the kindred grouping in the maintenance of law and order.

More generally, Wales was affected by European demographic trends. The fall in population after the Black Death increased the bargaining power of workers and led to the end of serfdom. Wage rates for hired labour rose. This interacted with a longer-term process by which serf labour declined in favour of money payments. Thus the long-established position of bondsmen was altered as they lost their character as serfs and instead became tenants, a source of revenue for landowners rather than labour. As tenants, they were able to participate in a rental economy in which the role of tenants, not the cohesion of the manor, became the central issue. Manors became less important than individual farms, a pattern that was to remain the case until today. That did not imply that the rural economy was without hardship and inequality, but instead that a major economic shift had important social consequences. Rent, not direct control, became more important, paving the way for a more enterprising and individualistic economy and society.

As almost all of the March was now in the hands of magnates, Wales was involved in the Wars of the Roses (1455–87), a protracted conflict between the houses of York and Lancaster over control of the throne that also involved bitter baronial feuds in much of the country. Henry VI was challenged by Richard, Duke of York, and then, more successfully, by the latter's son who became Edward IV in 1461. Nevertheless, much of the campaigning took place in England. There was a tendency to fight nearer the centre of power, but this does not explain the frequency of conflict in northern England. On balance, the northern counties were more contested and strategically more important. Northumberland in 1461–4, for example, was a much more significant theatre of war than Wales ever was, because of the strength of the Percys there, and the proximity of Scotland. It was easier to invade northern England than Wales from abroad. In addition, insofar as the Percy/Neville feud was an integral part of the fighting in 1459–71, Wales was a sideshow.

The Welsh, however, played a major role in the fighting, taking a prominent role in battles such as Mortimer's Cross (1469) and Bosworth (1485). In the first an army from west Wales under Owain and Jasper Tudor were defeated by the future Edward IV with men from the Mortimer estates. Welsh troops found themselves deployed on English battlefields in the service of Marcher lords. The fortunes of these lords varied with the course of the conflict. One prominent example was Sir William Herbert of Raglan Castle, a major supporter of the house of York. A descendant, like many Marcher figures, of both Anglo-Normans and Welsh lines, Herbert was the elder son of Sir William ap Thomas, the 'blue knight of Gwent', who had been knighted with Henry VI in 1426. His grandfather, Thomas ap Gwillim ap Jenkin, had married an English heiress.

Herbert acquired extensive military experience in France in the last stages of the Hundred Years War. When Edward IV became the first Yorkist monarch in 1461, Herbert was made Chief Justice and Chamberlain of south Wales. The same year, he was created Lord Herbert and granted the castle, town and lordship of Pembroke. In 1467, Herbert became Chief Justice of north Wales, and in 1468 he replaced Jasper Tudor as Earl of Pembroke and gained the lordship of Haverfordwest and the office of Chief Forester of Snowdon. Herbert's position was that of a trusty military henchman. He was made Steward of Brecknock Castle in 1461, Constable of Carmarthen and Cardigan Castles in 1467 and Constable of Conwy in 1468. He captured Harlech from Jasper Tudor that year. Raglan Castle was developed by Herbert, and he lived there in some state.

Pembroke was brought down in 1469. He marched an army of Welshmen into England to resist a Lancastrian rising encouraged by the Earl of Warwick, a renegade Yorkist, but was defeated at Edgecote and he and his brother were both then captured and executed. Many Welsh soldiers were also killed. Pembroke was buried at Tintern where he had been the abbey's steward. Pembroke's son, William, succeeded as 2nd Earl and in 1483 was appointed Justice of south Wales.

Pembroke was not the only victim of a post-battle decapitation. Owain Tudor was beheaded by the future Edward IV, after being taken prisoner at the battle of Mortimer's Cross in 1461. His second son, Jasper, had been created Earl of Pembroke by Henry VI, and he fought for the king at the first battle of St Albans in 1455, at the successful siege of Denbigh in 1460, at Mortimer's Cross in 1461, and in north Wales in 1468. When Henry VI was briefly restored in 1470, Jasper regained the Earldom of Pembroke and in 1471 was made commissioner of array for south Wales and the Marches and Constable of Gloucester Castle. The Lancastrian collapse forced him to flee to Brittany later that year with his nephew, Henry Tudor.

Another Marcher lord, Henry Stafford, 2nd Duke of Buckingham, Lord of Brecon, led a Welsh force into Herefordshire in 1483 in support of Henry Tudor and against Richard III whom he had recently helped to the throne. Buckingham had been rewarded with a Welsh power base: the posts of Chief Justice and Chamberlain of the Principality of Wales, and Constable and Steward of all the royal castles there and in the Marches. Nevertheless, he soon came to distrust Richard. Buckingham's invasion force was held up by 'the Duke of Buckingham's water' – floods on the Severn and Wye – and dispersed, leaving Buckingham to be captured and executed.

Welsh and Marcher positions and estates were thus used to reward key followers, even though the resulting manpower they raised fought, and died, in battlefields further afield. England replaced France and Scotland as the scene of Welsh campaigning, although it is not clear what effect this had on the soldiers.

THE TUDORS: UNION AND REFORMATION

In 1485, the lottery of military fortune and dynastic extinction brought Henry Tudor, who was a quarter Welsh and whose badge was the Welsh griffin, to the throne of England as Henry VII. His grandfather Owain, from the Tudors of Penmynydd, a leading Welsh official family in the Principality and, earlier, the leading servants of the rulers of Gwynedd prior to 1282, had married Henry V's French widow, Catherine; his father Edmund had in about 1455 married Margaret Beaufort, the heiress of the illegitimate Lancastrian line. The main line had been cut short in the Wars of the Roses and Henry Tudor, born in 1457 after the death of his father the previous year, was thus the unlikely* bearer of Lancastrian hopes against the house of York. He had taken refuge from the Yorkists, first in Brittany and then, after Richard III put pressure on its Duke, in France. Henry sailed from the Seine on 1 August 1485, landing at the entrance to Milford Haven on the 7th. The choice of landing site owed much to the position of Jasper Tudor, uncle of Henry Tudor, in the lordship of

Pembroke and provided the opportunity to build up support in Wales before attacking Richard III in England. This was necessary as Henry came with few troops. Invading England through Wales, Henry gained support, although some of it was conditional: Sir Rhys ap Thomas, a leading figure in Dyfed and the King's Chamberlain in west Wales, delayed until promised rewards. Henry reached Cardigan on 9 August, Welshpool on 13 August and Stafford on 17 August. Five days later, he defeated Richard at Bosworth. More crucially, Richard was killed, greatly weakening the Yorkists. This was not the end of the Wars of the Roses: there was a major Yorkist rebellion in 1487 that was defeated at the battle of Stoke, and lesser conspiracies thereafter. Nevertheless, Henry VII was now established on the throne.

Victory at Bosworth appeared to vindicate bardic prophecy about Welsh greatness, and when Henry landed at Milford Haven he promised to restore the Welsh to their liberties and free them from 'miserable servitudes'. The importance of Bosworth to the Welsh was as much psychological as anything else; there was a feeling that Llywelyn had been avenged and that new doors of opportunity had opened. Changes were indeed made: there were extensive concessions of the benefits of common law to the Welsh, while some Welshmen were appointed as bishops and took a major role in civil administration. Jasper Tudor regained his Earldom of Pembroke from the second earl, William Herbert, and also replaced him as Chief Justice of south Wales. Thereafter, Jasper Tudor played a prominent role in government, becoming Duke of Bedford and holding major posts, especially that of Lord Lieutenant of Ireland. Henry VII added the red dragon to the royal arms. In 1489, the title Prince of Wales was revived for Henry's first son who was significantly named Arthur. Following a precedent of the 1470s, a Council of Wales and the Marches under Prince Arthur covering Wales and nearby counties was established at Ludlow in Shropshire, although it was dominated by English administrators. Nevertheless, a political focus that was more immediate than distant London had been created for Wales. Opportunities were created for ambitious Welshmen, thus serving to develop an alliance between the Crown and the more active gentry.

Under Henry VII (1485–1509), Wales was far more peaceful than it had been for several decades. This was a peace that was less edgy than that after the Glyn Dŵr rising. Henry's background helped, but so also did the extent to which the Wars of the Roses had led to the forfeiture of many Marcher lordships and his own careful use of patronage. For example, Henry VII helped tie the Herbert interest to the crown through the marriage of Lady Elizabeth, the only child of William, 2nd Earl of Pembroke, to Charles Somerset (d. 1526), a key supporter. Somerset was made Constable of Montgomery Castle in 1504 and Baron Herbert in 1506, and the King's second son, Henry VIII (1509–47), made him Earl of Worcester in 1514. He used his positions to his own profit, forcing Richard Wyche, Abbot of Tintern (for which Somerset was the Steward) to complain about him to the Court of Star Chamber. A kinsman of Somerset, William Herbert of Ewyas, married Anne, sister of Henry VIII's sixth and last wife, Katherine Parr, and was granted monastic and royal estates, including Cardiff Castle.

Major change awaited the Reformation crisis. This led to greater concern about security and lawlessness and more acute sensitivity to the nature of government in regions remote from the centre of power in southern England. Wales was seen as exposed to possible Spanish and Irish intervention, while the Marcher lordships were regarded as badly administered, and the loyalty of some of the magnates was suspected, notably that of Sir Rhys ap Gruffydd, executed in 1531. Henry had already had Edward, 3rd Duke of Buckingham, executed on trumped up charges of treason in 1521. Henry VIII's legislation of 1536–43, the Acts of Union, assimilated all Wales into the English governmental system. In 1536, parliamentary representation was granted to the whole of Wales, although at less than the rate for England. Only one MP was allowed for each shire, in contrast to the two per county in England, while the boroughs in each shire were grouped and given just one MP, a contrast to the two MPs per borough in England. Welsh subjects were made equal to the English under the law, although the administrative language was to be English, and the Marcher lordships were grouped and converted into counties, and given representation in Parliament.

The new shires were Denbighshire, Montgomeryshire, Radnorshire, Breconshire and Monmouthshire, the last as judicially an English county. Glamorgan and Pembroke had been royal lordships governed as shires before 1536. The childless Jasper Tudor had left Pembroke to the then Duke of York, later Henry VIII. Glamorgan and Pembroke were officially recognized as shires in what was effectively an Act of Union in 1536. English inheritance practices, courts and county institutions were universally introduced. Welsh practices such as the gavelkind system of inheritance and the right of a lord to give shelter to a fleeing miscreant were abolished. Welsh land laws were abolished in 1543, but so also was legal discrimination against the Welsh.

The establishment of Justices of the Peace in Wales in 1536 gave the Welsh gentry an important measure of self-government. There were clerical and merchant JPs, but the majority were from the gentry, and the clerics were generally of gentry background. After 1542–3 Wales had its own system of courts, the Courts of Great Sessions, which had been in operation in the Principality since 1284, and were now extended. They lasted until 1830. As the Council of Wales and the Marches also continued, Wales was not governed in the same fashion as much of England, but Marcher independence had been destroyed and a uniform system of government created for Wales and for Monmouthshire. The English border counties were under the authority of the Council.

This was not a policy intended simply to control Wales. Instead, more generally, concern over uniformity and the determination to enforce change led to new claims for royal authority (albeit claims couched in the language of preserving continuity), the extension of royal power, the reorganisation of existing governmental practices, and the creation of new administrative agencies. In 1536, for example, Henry also resumed the special powers of the English palatinates. To a certain extent, the issue with the Marcher lordships was one of 'tidying up': many had already been absorbed into the crown with the Duchies of Lancaster and York, the Earldom of March, and the Neville lands.

The Council was given new energy by Rowland Lee, Bishop of Lichfield, who became its Lord President in 1534. His predecessor, the elderly John Veysey, Bishop of Exeter, had not been an energetic Lord President and he was blamed for a serious upsurge of lawlessness in the Marches that led to many complaints in the early 1530s. Lee was a trusted servant of Henry VIII and was close to Thomas Cromwell, the leading minister of the 1530s. In 1536, Lee boasted that 'all the thieves in Wales quake for feare'. Nevertheless, he was less than enthusiastic about the extension of the shire system and English justice, complaining that it would lead to 'one thief' trying another. Lee died in 1543. The Protestant William Herbert became Lord President in 1550 as a reward for his support of the Earl of Warwick, later Duke of Northumberland, against the Protector Somerset. He also became 1st Earl of Pembroke of the 2nd creation in 1551. Although Pembroke's star waned under the Catholic Queen Mary (1553–8), he avoided treason and was Lord President in 1555–8, thus helping to keep Wales peaceful during a difficult period.

The position of the President was consolidated under Sir Henry Sydney, who held the post for Elizabeth I from 1559 until his death in 1586. Sydney's previous posts had been as Vice-Treasurer (1556–9) and sole Lord Justice in Ireland (1558–9), and, as such, he had played a major role in military expeditions in Ulster and central Ireland. His presidency in Wales was very different. It was peaceful, and he was to claim that 'a better people to govern than the Welsh, Europe holdeth not'. Instead, Sydney was able during his period of office in Wales to return to Ireland as Lord Deputy. (Similarly, John Egerton, 1st Earl of Bridgewater, who was appointed Lord President in June 1631, did not visit Wales until May 1633 and did not make his public entrance until the autumn of 1634.)

As a result, the government of Wales was essentially left first – until the mid-Elizabethan period – largely to the border county gentry, and then to the Welsh gentry, many of whom sat on the Council. Sydney was succeeded by a major Welsh aristocrat, Henry Herbert, 2nd Earl of Pembroke, who held the Presidency until 1601. There were still serious problems with law and order. Sir James Perrot, Vice-Admiral (representative of the Admiralty) in Pembrokeshire between 1626 and 1637 complained, for example, about the activity of Welsh wreckers, who caused ships to run aground by placing lights on rocks. Nevertheless, there was nothing to match the disorder of the fifteenth century. Wales had ceased to be a 'marginal' area of the state.

The Welsh had identified themselves by their customary law, although the bards were more critical of the religious changes of the period than of the administrative innovations. The bards also lamented the decline of 'Welshness'. Equality of status, however, was the basis for a more mutually-beneficial relationship between the Welsh elite and the government. The preamble to the Act of Union of 1536 declared its aim to 'extirp[ate] . . . the sinister usages and customs' that caused differences between England and Wales, and it was declared that no Welshman could hold any post unless familiar with English, an objective that would have concentrated power where it already was: in the hands of gentry and clerics who could work with the English and were educated accordingly.

The Reformation had more of an immediate effect on the Welsh population than the administrative changes did. Although they were pretty run down by this time, the dissolution of monasteries, in 1536–40, and of chantries had an impact on landholding, substantially to the benefit of the local gentry who gained much of the land, and it also disrupted the fabric of many communities. Education and poor relief were affected. The abolition of shrines and pilgrimages in 1538 also hit well-established religious practices. Some continued. Despite the Council of Wales and the Marches considering its destruction in 1579, St Winifred's well in Flintshire was especially popular, as John Taylor noted in 1652 and Celia Fiennes in 1698.

The pre-Reformation Church had not been without vitality in Wales: several prominent clerics – for example Edward Vaughan, Bishop of St David's 1509–22 – were active figures. Yet although there were 47 monastic houses, there were only about 250 monks. It is appropriate that the ruins of Tintern dominate the modern image of the pre-Reformation Welsh Church, because the Cistercian house there was one of the very few with a strong monastic tradition. Most of the monasteries were poor and had few monks.

Church lands were seized under Henry VIII. The distribution or sale of them on easy terms to the nobility and, particularly, the gentry helped to bolster their loyalty. Rice Mansel (1487–1559), for instance, purchased Margam Abbey in 1540 and, under his grandson Sir Thomas (1556–1631), it became the principal seat of the Mansells. Their former seat, Oxwich Castle, in turn became less important. Sir Edward Carne took over the lands of Ewenni Priory, the Wynnes of Melai those of Maenan Abbey. Other families that benefited included the Herberts and Stradlings. Henry, 2nd Earl of Worcester, was granted Tintern Abbey, which had been dissolved in 1536: this helped consolidate the regional power base of the Earl who already controlled Chepstow and Raglan Castle.

Enthusiasm for the Reformation was limited. There was little sign of Protestantism in Wales under Henry VIII, in part because trade with the Low Countries and Germany, one of the major routes for the transmission of the new religion in both England and Scotland, was limited. Furthermore, town life was not prominent, and early Protestantism very much had an urban milieu. There were only four known executions for Protestantism in Wales under Henry or Mary. Robert Ferrar, Bishop of St David's 1544–55, who was burnt in Carmarthen in 1555, was a Cambridge-educated Yorkshireman who was opposed to Welsh-speakers. In Caernarvonshire, the purge of married priests under Mary claimed only five clerics, two of whom preferred to abandon their wives. The absence of a Bible and Prayer Book in Welsh was important in limiting support for the Reformation. Areas of Catholicism remained. Nevertheless, there was no equivalent to the Catholic opposition to the Reformation that existed in England, Ireland and Scotland, in part because change in Wales was so poorly implemented. There was no Catholic rising, as there was in northern England in 1536 and 1569 and Cornwall in 1549; nor indeed a rising against Mary's marriage to Philip II of Spain in 1553, as in Kent, Devon and the west Midlands. During Mary's reign the ambitious Lewis Owen, Sheriff of Merioneth, was ambushed and killed by yeomen as a protest (not for religious reasons as far as can be seen), but opposition was not more widespread.

The stability of Wales, certainly compared to the north of England, was also clear during the reign of Elizabeth I (1558–1603), though the government was concerned on occasion: there were rumours, for example, about plans by William, 3rd Earl of Worcester, to rebel in Wales in 1569 when the northern Earls rose, but he didn't, and instead proved a loyal servant.

The translation of the Bible into Welsh helped to sustain a sense of national identity. The Welsh accepted the Reformation, but not the English language; thanks to the acceptance of the former, Wales did not become a security problem and source of Protestant phobias and was spared the fate of Ireland. It also, in this period, lacked a religious and ecclesiastical distinctiveness akin to Presbyterianism in Scotland and the Catholicism of most of the Irish population. A translation of the Prayer Book and the New Testament commissioned by Elizabeth I was published in 1567 and William Morgan's readily-comprehensible translation of the entire Bible appeared in 1588, although the metropolitan dominance of Britain was such that it had to be printed in London: by law only certain presses could publish Bibles anyway. In his Latin dedication to Elizabeth I, Morgan emphasised the value of official support of the Welsh language. Morgan had grown up at Tŷ Mawr Wybrnant near Penmachno in Gwynedd, although the sixteenth-century farmhouse there possibly postdates him.

Thanks to the translation, Welsh could be the official language of public worship and religious life in general, and the clergy had no need to catechise and preach in English. The Welsh language could develop from its medieval oral and manuscript characteristics into a culture of print. Morgan was subsequently an active bishop of first Llandaff and then St Asaph and his career testified to the energising possibilities of the Reformation. Other bishops, however, left a less happy reputation, although this was also true of the clergy in England. Although not without merits, William Hughes, Bishop of St Asaph between 1573 and 1600, became notorious for his pluralism, and was accused of corruptly leasing out episcopal lands. Hughes's career illustrated the degree to which the literate Welsh now looked toward England. Educated at Cambridge, where he became a fellow, he was for long chaplain to the Duke of Norfolk and toward the end of his career he sought translation to Exeter. If Welshmen sought careers in England with increasing success, some senior Welsh positions were still held by Englishmen, although English occupation of Welsh sees did not become significant in (south) Wales until *c.* 1615. Hugh Bellot, who obtained livings in Flintshire in 1584, and was Bishop of Bangor between 1585 and 1595, was English but the Bellot family had Welsh associations. His predecessor and successor were Welsh. The foundation of Jesus College, Oxford in 1571 strengthened the synergy between developing Protestantism, the English language, a habit of looking to England, and social mobility: a gift from Hugh Price of Brecon, whose family was a major beneficiary of the dissolution of the monasteries, the college operated as a university for Wales, and many Welsh clerics and gentlemen passed through it. The foundation of a series of schools – at Abergavenny, Bangor, Brecon, Carmarthen and Ruthin – from the 1530s to the 1570s was also important in linking education, Protestantism and the English language.

Several, including Christ's College Brecon, Friar's School Bangor, and Abergavenny School, were based on monastic holdings.

Although the Welsh Catholics who were persecuted under Elizabeth would not have appreciated the point, control and influence in Tudor Wales were decreasingly exercised through the use of the threat of force, though William Morgan's quarrels with some of his parishioners led both to violence in 1590 and to Morgan carrying a pistol underneath his cassock. More generally, family and kindred feuds were both bitter and sustained.

Notwithstanding, many castles were abandoned, and fell into disrepair and ruin, while others were enhanced not with new fortifications but with comfortable and splendid internal 'spaces', particularly long galleries, as at Raglan Castle for the Earl of Worcester, Powis Castle for Sir Edward Herbert in 1592–3, and Carew Castle for Sir John Perrot (d. 1592). In contrast, a 1627 survey of Conwy Castle revealed that it was in a poor state. Beaumaris was described as 'utterlie decayed' in 1609, but was later repaired by the Bulkeleys. Military training and a coterie of armed followers became less important to landowners.

Welsh society as a whole was far from affluent, but was increasingly prosperous, although some sixteenth-century developments were prefigured long before: Marcher lords carried off big profits from south Wales, especially through wool and cattle, while upwardly mobile Welshmen had for long been educated at Oxbridge or at the Inns of Court in London. Sixteenth-century wills suggested much prosperity, with their description of household contents and account of house rebuilding. As in England, the Tudor age was a period of rising population, from about 226,000 in the 1540s to about 342,000 in 1670; and of expanding trade and agriculture. Formerly common land was enclosed, sometimes illegally as by Sir Thomas Myddelton at Chirk in the 1610s. The area of cultivation was extended. Cattle and sheep were driven to English markets, especially London. This could involve ferries across the Bristol Channel: from Sully, near Cardiff, to Uphill in Somerset, and from Beachley to Aust. Bristol was supplied from south Wales with butter and meat. Welsh cloth was taken to Shrewsbury for finishing. In the late seventeenth century, grain exports from Cardiganshire became considerable.

The role of the market economy became more insistent and increasingly affected areas formerly characterised by subsistence agriculture and poverty. The more fertile lands of south Wales ensured that the counties of

Pembroke, Carmarthen, Glamorgan and Brecknock accounted for nearly half the population. Denbighshire was also well populated. Upland Radnorshire and Merionethshire had the lowest population. The high prices and long-term inflation that helped landowners also hit the poor, leading to an increase in destitution and vagrancy. Agricultural improvement, such as enclosures and the use of lime on acidic soil, brought more wealth to the landowners. The lot of the poor, however, was more difficult. Aside from higher rents and prices, they were affected by the pressure of a rising population on limited land and food. Harvest failures posed particular problems in the 1620s and 1630s.

Landowners also gained wealth from the mining that took place on their estates. Much coal went to supply local needs, but an increasing amount was exported. Swansea's annual coal exports rose from about 1,800 tons in the 1550s to about 7,700 in 1640, and the population there rose substantially, fed by migration from within Wales. Henry VIII supported iron and lead mining near Llantrisant. Lead mining in Cardiganshire developed under Elizabeth I. Copper, iron and slate production also expanded. The first copper smelter near Neath, built by the Mines Royal in about 1584, depended on water power from the Aberdulais Falls, although the copper ore was imported from Cornwall. This was part of the slow process by which the economy in Britain was becoming more integrated. Although the cost and difficulty of transport limited developments, each such move encouraged a sense of interdependency.

Water power from the Angidy brook encouraged the development of iron wire production from the mid-1560s near the ruined Tintern Abbey. The furnace was fed with charcoal made from local timber, and by 1700 there was a second furnace on the site and a second forge nearby. At the close of the seventeenth century, the well-travelled Celia Fiennes visited north-east Wales: 'there are great coale pitts – they have great wheeles that are turned with horses that draw up the water and so draine the Mines which would else be overflowed so as they could not dig the coale; they have also engines that draw up their coale in sort of baskets like hand barrows which they wind up like a bucket in a well, for their mines are dug down through a sort of well and sometymes its pretty low before they come to the coales . . . quarrys of stone, copper and iron mines and salt hills'. Despite the growth in mining, traditional agricultural processing industries were more important, especially those using animal skin and wool: leather and cloth-making.

Although industrial and commercial production were important, they produced neither a large class of craftsmen nor an important urban sector: only about nine per cent of the population lived in towns, and the small towns would today be seen as villages. They were all closely involved in the surrounding rural economy. In many respects the most important Welsh towns were Chester, Shrewsbury, Bristol and London. The role of coastal trade made Bristol and Chester particularly important to Wales, while droving and pack horses brought Welsh goods to Marcher markets in Chester, Oswestry, Shrewsbury, Ludlow and Bristol. The most successful Welsh merchants worked abroad, Richard Clough (d. 1570) making a large fortune as a merchant in Antwerp, although he married in Wales and built several houses there. There was no national census to provide precise population figures until 1801, but the largest Welsh towns in the sixteenth and early seventeenth centuries were probably Brecon, Carmarthen and Wrexham. Swansea's population in 1670 was only about 1,800. It derived much of its importance from being a port, as also did Cardigan, Carmarthen, Haverfordwest, Pembroke and Tenby. Fiennes was unimpressed with 'Flint town; its a very ragged place, many villages in England are better, the houses all thatched and stone walls but so decayed that in many places ready to tumble down; there was a Town Hall such a one as it was; it was at a session tyme when I was there which showed it at its prime'.

The newly-wealthy gentry built prestigious houses, such as Sir David Williams's Gwernyfed, Robert Wynn's Plas Mawr, Sir John Trevor's Plas Teg, and Sir Thomas Morgan's Ruperra. They entertained liberally, showed great interest in genealogical studies and sought to adopt a code of aristocratic conduct. They were very interested in education which secured their gentility, distinguished them from the rest of the community and provided valuable legal skills. Some discarded Welsh and ceased to patronise bardic culture, but many did not, and most of the gentry were far from wealthy. Indeed Wales was noted for its poor gentry.

THREE

From Seventeenth Century to the Industrial Revolution

The Seventeenth Century

The seventeenth century was to bring civil war again to Wales, although it suffered far less grievously than the other parts of Britain. There was criticism of the policies of Charles I (1625–49) in the 1620s and 1630s and, in particular, of the activities of the Council of Wales and the Marches, which was to be suspended by Parliament in 1641. Sir James Perrot, MP for Haverfordwest, attacked royal policies in Parliament, condemning financial impositions in 1614, the proposed Spanish (Catholic) marriage of the future Charles I in 1621 and the Church policies of William Laud in 1628. However, criticism was far less serious than that elsewhere, especially in Scotland. The Ship Money levied without parliamentary authority was mostly paid and without particular difficulties. Pirates were a problem along the Welsh coast.

Furthermore, the Arminian Church policies of Charles and William Laud, Archbishop of Canterbury, which struck critics as crypto-Catholic did not lead to serious distress, especially outside the major towns. This may reflect not only apathy, but a measure of support for the policies. In 1639–40, when Charles campaigned against the rebellious Scots, he was able to raise troops in Wales.

The failure of these campaigns forced Charles to turn to Parliament: he had ruled without one since 1629. Initially, Welsh MPs joined in the widespread attacks on royal prerogatives and policies in what was to be the Long Parliament, but, as the crisis gathered pace and more radical solutions were advocated in 1641, they increasingly rallied to the king. The onset of civil war in England and Wales in 1642 found the overwhelming majority of the Welsh loyal: support for Parliament was strongest in Pembrokeshire. The Welsh gentry both inherently conservative and, on the whole, beneficiaries of royal policies over the previous century and a half, were overwhelmingly Royalist and there was no large urban environment within which support for Parliament and Puritanism could develop. Prominent landowners, such as the Catholic Henry, 5th Earl of Worcester, provided the king with much support, in his case with large sums of money. His eldest son, Edward Somerset, a Catholic, was made Lieutenant-General and played a major role in raising support in Glamorgan and Monmouthshire.

Royalists were concerned mostly to defend the established order in Church, State and Society: the peers and gentry thought their position bound up with that of the king, although Philip Herbert, Earl of Pembroke, supported Parliament, as did the Myddletons of Chirk. The bulk of the population, at least initially, seem to have been largely apathetic and to have known little of the issues at stake, not least because English was the language of opposition to Charles I, although the popular poetry that was written in Wales favoured the Royalist cause. The experience of Puritan government in the 1650s was to make this a much stronger sentiment.

Wales produced large numbers of men and much money for Charles, and Welsh troops, especially infantry, played a major role both in operations against nearby targets, particularly Gloucester, and in more distant fields. Many Welsh soldiers served Charles in the Midlands. Defeat at the battle of Naseby in 1645 was particularly fatal for the Welsh infantry.

Initially fighting within Wales was confined to the south-west, where south Pembrokeshire supported Parliament. Both the towns and the local gentry backed Parliament. The area had strong links with Bristol, then a Parliamentarian stronghold, and also traditions of political and religious opposition to Charles. Tenby and

Haverfordwest fell to the Royalists with little resistance in 1643, but Pembroke was reinforced by a Parliamentary fleet in 1643 and much of the county was retaken in the spring of 1644. Parliamentary forces then advanced to capture Cardiganshire and Carmarthen from which they were driven in the summer of 1644. Fighting swayed to and fro until after the Parliamentary victory at Colby Heath on 1 August 1645 when the impact of Parliamentary success elsewhere helped to produce triumph in south-west Wales.

In November 1643, much of north-east Wales was overrun by Parliamentary forces intent on closing a route for reinforcements from Ireland, but they were driven back by troops from Ireland in December, and it was not until the summer of 1644 that the Parliamentarians made a major impact again in the region, capturing Oswestry in June, raiding Welshpool in August, capturing Montgomery Castle on 5 September and defeating the Royalists outside Montgomery on 18 September, the largest Civil War battle in Wales; Powis Castle fell to a night attack the following month. Monmouth had been captured the previous month, but was regained by the Royalists in November. Meanwhile, Royalist support was declining, due to the burden of the conflict and Charles's use of Irish troops. This led in the summer of 1645 to the raising of the 'Peaceable Army' in south Wales, in an attempt to force concessions from Charles. The fall of nearby Royalist bases in England, Shrewsbury, Bristol and Chester, between February 1645 and February 1646, was crucial. Royalist confidence in Wales and the Welsh economy were undermined, and in the autumn of 1645 the Royalist position in south Wales collapsed with mass defections. The castles were left in Royalist hands, but they fell to the remorseless pressure of superior Parliamentary forces: Chepstow and Monmouth in October, Caernarfon and Beaumaris in June 1645, Aberystwyth in April 1646, Raglan in August, Conwy in November, Holt Castle in January 1647, and Harlech finally surrendering on 16 March 1647, the last Royalist stronghold on mainland Britain.

In 1648, Royalists and dissatisfied Parliamentarians launched the second Civil War. There were risings in Anglesey, Caernarfon and Merioneth, but only that in south Wales was serious, though it was rapidly crushed. John Poyer, the Governor of Pembroke, declared for Charles I in March 1648 and at Pwllcrochan on 29 March defeated a force sent by sea from Bristol to restore order. The rebels moved into Glamorgan, having defeated another Parliamentary force in an ambush at Llandeilo. Swansea and Neath fell in early May, but the advance on

Cardiff was blocked by Colonel Horton from the garrison at Brecon. The rebels attacked on 8 May but the more experienced Parliamentarians defeated the larger force, largely due to their superior cavalry and dragoons, capturing much of it. Several of the Royalist officers were executed.

This defeat was followed up by the arrival of a large Parliamentary force under Oliver Cromwell, his first military operation in Wales. He stormed the town of Chepstow on 11 May, leaving the castle to be stormed on 25 May after the walls had been breached by heavy cannon. Cromwell pushed on into Pembrokeshire, capturing Pembroke on 11 July and ending the rebellion in south Wales. The Caernarvonshire rebellion under Sir John Owen had been defeated at Y Dalar Hir on the coast road east of Penrhyn on 5 June. Anglesey declared for Charles I in July, but the Parliamentarians successfully invaded in late September, won an engagement at Red Hill west of Beaumaris on 1 October and captured the castle next day by threatening to hang their prisoners. As in the first Civil War, the upland areas of central Wales, especially Merionethshire and Breconshire, were largely peaceful.

The Royalist defeat was followed by the creation of a new ruling order. The 'slighting' of castles, for example the demolition of Raglan's Great Tower, was a potent symbol of the fall of aristocratic power. Other castles slighted included Abergavenny, Aberystwyth, Flint, Laugharne, Montgomery, Pembroke, Rhuddlan and Ruthin.

Charles I was beheaded as a traitor in 1649 and, as in England, the Interregnum (1649–60) was a period of great uncertainty, although there was less disruption to the social than to the religious order. Nevertheless, prominent Royalists such as Edward Somerset, who had succeeded his father as 6th Earl and 2nd Marquis of Worcester in 1646, found their lands sequestrated. Oliver Cromwell was granted Worcester's Monmouthshire lands. Worcester was imprisoned in the Tower of London in 1652–4. His son, however, abandoned Catholicism and became a Cromwellian MP as plain Mr Herbert. Seized by the Parliamentarians in October 1644, Powis Castle was not restored to Catholic ownership until the Restoration of Charles II.

The composition of the Commissions of Peace changed markedly. Much of the local gentry was purged from county government in 1646 or after the second Civil War in 1648, although many Royalists who had declared for Parliament in 1645–6 and avoided involvement in 1648 continued to hold office. Nevertheless, the replacement of many traditional local rulers allowed others experience of power. Most were from the lesser gentry, but there were also new men, most prominently Cromwell's friend Philip Jones, who was a key figure in south Wales. Born in Swansea, he became its Governor (1645) and a colonel (1646), Governor of Cardiff Castle (1648), a MP from 1650, and a member of the Council of State (1653). Thanks, in part, to his alacrity in embezzlement, not least as one of the Commissioners responsible for Puritan evangelism, Jones gained much land, including Fonmon Castle, and survived the Restoration of Charles II, becoming Sheriff of Glamorgan. This was very challenging to traditional assumptions about power and authority. So, also, was the situation in Anglesey where the widespread participation by the gentry in the 1648 rising led to the imposition of government by outsiders. Several key heiresses in the period were married to Cromwellian military figures, such as John Carter and George Twistleton, a challenge to the local elite, although one lessened by the ability of such figures to join this elite.

The Interregnum witnessed a major attempt to spread radical Puritanism. Under an Act of 1650 for 'the Better Propagation of the Gospel in Wales', 71 Commissioners were instructed to organise the evangelism of Wales; 278 Anglican clerics were dispossessed, mostly in 1650, their tithes and livings placed at the disposal of the Commissioners, who helped themselves to some of it; and itinerant Puritan preachers were appointed. One of the more prominent was Vavasor Powell, who had received a bullet wound during the war and then thought himself called by a heavenly voice: 'I have chosen thee to preach the gospel'. The Commissioners also founded more than seventy free schools. This religious radicalism was intended to create a new socio-religious order that some supporters hoped would serve as an example for the rest of Britain.

Radical political and religious ideas, such as those of the Quakers who were active from the mid-1650s, aroused widespread antipathy and most of the Welsh remained attached to the Anglican Church. Such allegiance could take ugly forms: the Quaker evangelist Alice Birkett was stripped naked and stoned in Llandaff churchyard. Opposition to the corruption and objectives of the Commissioners helped turn support from the republican regime, thus further forcing it to rely on an unpopular minority.

The cohesion of this minority was shattered by differences over religion, for example in response to the Quakers, and politics. Cromwell's decision to become Lord Protector in 1653 was especially divisive and greatly angered Welsh Puritans, such as Vavasor Powell, who saw monarchy on earth as an anti-Christian abomination. Many came to support the millenarian Fifth Monarchy party. Nevertheless, although uncomfortable with Cromwell, these radicals were opposed to a Stuart restoration, and thus Interregnum governments turned to them when threatened, as in 1659. This increased support for a restoration.

Widespread conservatism was to ensure that the Restoration of Charles II in 1660 was generally popular, although there were a number of republican plots in the 1660s and the clampdown on Nonconformist preaching led to the imprisonment of preachers such as Powell and many Quakers. One hundred and thirty Puritan ministers lost their livings, and the free schools established in the 1650s were closed. Nonconformists were often harshly treated under the Penal Laws. The ejected clergy became leaders of dissenting congregations which ensured that there was no unity in Welsh Protestant attitudes but, instead, a divided and frequently bitter community, prone to fears about insurrection, conspiracy and persecution. Some leading families, such as the Mansells, supported the Dissenters, and thus it was more than a creed of working people and those lacking 'respectability' and 'position'.

Royalists, such as Worcester, were restored to all or most of their estates in 1660. His son, a supporter of the Restoration of Charles II, became Warden of the Forest of Dean and Lord Lieutenant of Gloucestershire, Hereford-shire and Monmouthshire. The Council of Wales and the Marches had also been restored in 1660 and in 1672, Henry Somerset, the Mr Herbert of the Interregnum years, 3rd Marquis of Worcester since 1667, became its Lord President. He helped to keep Wales loyal during the Exclusion Crisis of 1679–81, was advanced to the title of Duke of Beaufort in 1682 and, as Lord President, staged a semi-regal progress in 1684. Worcester was an opponent of the Dissenters, but was in turn feared as a sponsor of Catholicism.

From the Restoration, until the impact of industrialis-ation, Wales was a particularly conservative part of Britain, overwhelmingly Anglican, and strongly Royalist under the restored Stuarts, Charles II (1660–85) and James II (1685–8), although support for the crown did erode during the scares about Catholic conspiracies, such as the Popish Plot of 1678–9. Wales was also keenly Tory until the mid-eighteenth century. Despite the presence of Whigs and Dissenters, there was no equivalent to the Covenanter risings in Scotland or to the risings against James II and VII in England and Scotland in 1688. Gentry confidence was seen in extensive building, for example the major expansion of Tredegar House by Sir William Morgan in the 1670s and extensive work at Powis Castle. Parliamentary representation in the early eighteenth century was dominated by the Tories. Excluding Monmouthshire, the 21,000 Welsh voters returned 21 Tory to 3 Whig MPs in 1713, and in 1715, a year of Whig victory, the figures were still 15 and 9.

When William III seized power with the 'Glorious Revolution' of 1688–9 he turned against some of the most prominent supporters of James II and VII. The Catholic William, 1st Marquess of Powis fled into exile with James, and his estates were granted to Dutch followers of William who were made Duke of Portland and Earl of Rochford. However, in part because resistance to the Revolution in Wales was perfunctory (unlike in Ireland or Scotland), there was no attempt to transform Welsh politics and society as there was in Ireland from the 1690s and in the Scottish Highlands after the suppression of the 1745 Jacobite rising. Indeed, the Powis estates were restored to the 2nd Marquess in 1722. The suppression of the Council of Wales and the Marches in 1689 was scarcely comparable to developments in Scotland and Ireland, and did not lead to any sense of loss. Thus the 'Glorious Revolution' of 1688–9 was not followed by a dispossession like the Act of Union with Scotland in 1707 or the destruction of the Catholic position in Ireland. This was important to the stability of Wales over the following century, a stability that was only to be disrupted subsequently by the pressures of industrialisation and social change. The exclusion from power of the Catholic and High Tory aristocrats whom Charles II and James II had favoured helped to lessen political tension in Wales, and encouraged the development of a new political world, one that was more dominated by the gentry.

THE EIGHTEENTH CENTURY

Wales was dominated by its Anglican gentry. Compared to England and Scotland, the peerage was sparse and relatively unimportant and the gentry clearly dominant, although the Dukes of Beaufort controlled Monmouth. Relatively few of the gentry were promoted into the peerage into this period, although the Mansells were in 1711; and several major lines had come to an end, the male line of the Earls of Pembroke in 1683. Gentry families such as the Wynns of Wynnstay, who dominated Denbighshire, and the Morgans of Tredegar, who had estates in Monmouthshire and Breconshire, and also their feuds, were central to Welsh politics. In Cardiganshire, the vicious and unpopular Sir Herbert Lloyd, MP 1761–8, had serious disputes with Wilmot, 1st Earl of Lisburne, the Pryses of Gogerddan and the Powells of Nanteos, on issues such as control of the Surveyorship of Royal Mines in Wales and the arranging of local elections. In 1755, Lloyd was dismissed as a JP for abusing his position. The bitter mid-century electoral history of the county was essentially a matter of personal and family divisions: ideology played little role. In Anglesey, the Whig challenge to Tory hegemony between 1689 and 1730 was an aspect of the challenge by local squires to the dominant Bulkeley family, and was exacerbated by the personal rivalry of Richard, 4th Viscount Bulkeley and Owen Meyrick MP. Carmarthenshire was dominated by the Vaughans of Golden Grove until the male line of the main branch died out in 1713 with the death of the 3rd Earl of Carbery. Tories were divided over whether to support the Jacobite Pretender (the exiled Stuart), but this became less serious an issue after the failure of the 1715 rising, although it revived in the 1740s.

The quarrelsome gentry elite was more closely identifying itself with a sense of British identity. At their level there was a decline in the use of Welsh, and English cultural norms and customs had a growing appeal. This was true, for example, of architecture and landscape gardening. New building, such as Nanteos for the Powells, and enhancements, such as the stately rooms at Chirk Castle for the Myddletons and the ballroom at Powis Castle for the Herberts, were produced in what were established British aristocratic styles. This was also true of the gardens. William Emes advised Philip Yorke at Erddig between 1767 and 1789, creating hanging gardens and 'natural' clumps of trees. He was also responsible for the landscaping at Chirk Castle and Powis Castle, and for work at Wimpole in England.

The Welsh gentry increasingly intermarried with their English counterparts, while a greater number of heirs were educated in England. This was even more true of the aristocracy. George, 2nd Earl of Powis 1755–1801, who was accused by John Byng of extravagance 'in the prodigalities of London and in driving high phaetons up St James's Street', gave little attention to Powis Castle. At the same time, though, possibly over 80 or even 90 per cent of the population of Wales used Welsh as the medium of communication.

The social divide was captured by the half-Welsh William Jones (1746–94), later famous as a founder of modern linguistics. In 1775, he visited market day at Llandeilo and emphasised a sense of contrast:

I could not help fancying myself in a Flemish town; it was at least wholly unlike an English one, as the manners, dress, and countenances of the people are entirely different from ours. I speak of the lower sort, for the gentry are not in any respect distinguishable from us.

What was life like for the bulk of the population? It was similar in Wales to that of other European peasant societies of the period. That does not mean that the conditions of life should be neglected: it is all too easy to see life in the past in modern terms, to look for similarities and to underrate differences. In fact, the experience of life was totally different. The closeness of death shaped both individual and collective experiences. There was still joy and pleasure, exultation and exhilaration, but there was also an ever-present threat of death, disease, injury and pain. Alongside long-lasting individuals, there were lives quickly cut short, in the case of women especially in childbirth and for children particularly through infection. Social structures were also different to today's. Marriage was far more important to household formation. Bar occasional bigamies, wife sales, and aristocratic Bills of Divorce, marriage was irreversible, and ended only with the death of one of the partners. Most childbearing was within marriage. Despite the absence of effective contraceptives, recorded illegitimacy rates were low, very low by modern standards, although it is impossible to say how much illegitimacy was concealed by infanticide. Marriages were also generally late, so that childbearing was postponed until an average of over ten years past puberty, which itself occurred later than today.

Defences against disease remained flimsy. Medical knowledge was limited and, due to poor nutrition and a lack of warm, dry housing, resistance was low. There was no comparison to modern suppositions that there should be a cure for everything – only folk remedies, prayer and palliatives. Alcohol was the major painkiller. There was much trust in quack medicines and herbal remedies. Troubled by failing eyesight, John Meller, who bought Erdigg from the bankrupt Joshua Edisbury in 1716, was recommended the herb Eyebright by his sister: 'I had the distilled water of it and thought it no way unpleasant being sweetened with sugar. You may also make a tea of it or have it dried'.

Crowded housing conditions, especially the sharing of beds, helped spread diseases, particularly respiratory infections. Sanitary practices were also a problem. Washing in clean water was limited, most people wore the same clothes for as long as they could, and louse infestation was serious. Although outer clothes were worn for long periods, and were not washable, those who could afford it wore linen and cotton shifts next to their skin, and these shifts could be regularly laundered. Good footwear was similarly available to few. Celia Fiennes recorded 'the inhabitants go barefoote and bare leg'd'. Bed bugs and rats were major problems. By modern standards, breath and skin must have been repellent.

It is difficult to recreate the smell and dirt of the period. Ventilation and drainage were limited. Humans lived close to animals and dunghills, and this hit health: storage of manure near buildings was hazardous and could contaminate the water supply; effluent from undrained privies and animal pens flowed across streets and into houses through generally porous walls; privies with open soil pits lay directly alongside dwellings and under bedrooms. Pump and river water was often contaminated, encouraging disease.

Working conditions were also tough. Agricultural workers were exposed to the elements and worked very long hours. Many tasks had to be accomplished by hand: mechanical tools were limited. Places of work within buildings were often damp, poorly lit and badly ventilated. Many working processes were dangerous – this was true of construction, fishing, mining and mineral processing.

Miners suffered death and injury from floods, falls, and underground explosions while working by candlelight. There was much poverty, and the price and availability of food were serious issues, leading in 1740 to dangerous food riots in Flintshire and Wrexham.

Wales lacked centralising institutions or social, ecclesiastical or legal arrangements corresponding with its linguistic distinctiveness. Nevertheless, there was a clear sense of identity, expressed in part through hostility to outsiders. Thus, in 1735 John Campbell of Calder (Cawdor), MP for Pembrokeshire and possessor of estates there and in Scotland, wrote to his son

On Sunday there came here . . . two Highlanders in highland clothes without breeches, with long swords and each a pistol stuck in his girdle, they brought your uncle Philipps eight dogs . . . The Highlanders came by Shrewsbury, through Montgomeryshire and Cardiganshire. The people in England were very civil to them and pleased with their dress, but when they came some miles into Wales the people were afraid of them and the folks of the inns would not have given them lodging. They were forced when they came into an inn to say that they would pay for what they had and to behave themselves civilly and so doing, they would not be turned out of a public house, saying this with their pistols in their hands

frighted the folks into compliance, or else they must
have lain under the hedges, and may be got no victuals,
but this was among the Wild Welsh; in our part of the
country [Pembrokeshire] they know a little better.

The Welsh could indeed be wild. Distant Cardiganshire
was notorious for gangs of brigands in the Ystwyth
valley and for polygamy.

In 1776, Jabez Fisher, an American Quaker traveller,
recorded of Shropshire, 'Call the People in this country
Welsh and you offend them: go into Wales and you can
offer them no greater insult than to call them English. Is
this Patriotism? Tis Love of one's own Country'. In fact,
due to intermarriage and to migration, the divide was far
less clear-cut.

In the eighteenth century, scholars and antiquaries
were carving out a Welsh identity as descendants of the
Ancient Britons (as opposed to the modern British) in
terms of the ancient language and history of Wales.
Some of their claims were totally spurious, notably those
made by the remarkable reviver of the bardic craft,
Edward Williams (1747–1826), but this was scarcely
uncommon in comparable developments elsewhere in
Europe. Welsh circles in London played a major role in
this cultural revival. Thomas Jones (1743–1803), one of

the leading Welsh painters of the period, was born in Radnorshire, studied at Jesus College, Oxford and from 1762 lived for many years in London, following the style of his teacher Richard Wilson. He largely painted Welsh scenery. The Cymmrodorion and Gwyneddigion Societies in London met regularly and played an important role in the revival of the *eisteddfod*. The prize offered by the London Gwyneddigion Society in 1789 for the best long poem was an important spur, and they encouraged literary developments in Wales, especially the writings of David Thomas (1759–1822). This impetus took over from the now weak bardic tradition, and provided a new form of public culture.

This clear sense of identity based on the Welsh language and on the sense of the Welsh past had no political expression or consequences. Wales was not treated in any distinctive fashion and presented no particular problems for London ministries. There was no nationalist movement. There were also no particular agencies for the government of Wales: no equivalent, for example, to the Secretary of State for Scotland. The Council of Wales and the Marches had been abolished in 1689: the new government of William III preferred to centralise power in London and not to rely on Welsh aristocrats, most of whom were Tories. New initiatives, such as income tax, the Ordnance Survey, and the census at the close of the eighteenth century and the beginning of the nineteenth, were introduced without qualification for Wales. London-based institutions such as the Customs and the Excise encompassed Wales. There was nothing to match the distinctive Scottish legal and religious system, nor any attempt to match such distinctiveness.

Wales was also of scant importance in political terms. Its 24 MPs (27 if Monmouthshire is included) were far fewer than those from Cornwall, and formed only a small portion of the 558 MPs elected after the Act of Union with Scotland in 1707, so the Welsh MPs no longer constituted a distinct political interest at Westminster. The use of single-member constituencies, as opposed to the English norm of two members, lessened the Welsh role. Monmouthshire, however, had two MPs for the county and one for Monmouth. The Welsh boroughs mirrored the English franchises, with corporation, freemen, and scot and lot electorates (where franchise depended on payment of the poor rate or the Church rate), and the franchise in the county seats was, as in England, the possession of freehold property valued at 40 shillings per year. However, the poverty of Wales and the small size of the population were such that the total electorate in 1790 was fewer than 19,000. This compared with about 300,000 in England. Wrexham, the largest town, was not a parliamentary borough. There were relatively few parliamentary contests in Wales and the number of these fell.

In terms of extra-parliamentary politics, despite riots as in Wrexham in 1715 and 1740 and in Carmarthen in 1755, Wales was relatively docile. During the Jacobite crises, Wales was essentially quiet. Although there was a Welsh Jacobite tradition among leading gentry in the north and the south, it did not lead to rebellion. There was nothing to compare with the Scottish risings of 1715 and 1745. There was Welsh support for John Wilkes, a prominent critic of George III in the 1760s, and some criticism of the decision to use force against the American Patriots in the 1770s, but this was not unique to Wales. These ideas looked towards Welsh radicalism in the nineteenth century, but their impact in the eighteenth while considerable was far more limited. Radicals such as Watkin Lewis and Robert Morris pursued their careers outside Wales, but, in the 1780s, interest in parliamentary reform increased. The Glamorgan by-election of 1789 produced much anti-aristocratic propaganda, directed against the Duke of Beaufort, Lord Vernon, and Lord Mountstuart, but the successful challenge, on behalf of Thomas Wyndham, was mounted by a group of independent gentry led by Thomas Mansell Talbot. The 1790s, however, produced a change as the example of the French Revolution encouraged the development and expression of radical thought.

No monarch visited Wales in the eighteenth century, but then none visited Ireland, Scotland or the north of England either. Wales, especially north Wales, also, saw very little of the army. Minor detachments from regiments stationed in England were usually found only at Carmarthen, Aberystwyth and Aberdovey, and their major function was to support the Customs and Excise and prevent smuggling. 'Wrecking', looting the cargoes of wrecked ships, and in some cases luring them to their destruction, was a problem in some coastal areas. When the French sent an invasion force to Pembrokeshire in 1797, it was defeated by local volunteer forces, and the garrison in the fort at Fishguard Harbour had only three rounds of ammunition. Other fortified positions, such as Beaumaris and Conwy, had been allowed to decay since the 1650s.

Wales was also open to English investment. The Act of Union had contributed to a sense that Wales was a safe place to invest. Bristol financiers developed copper works near Swansea from 1717, as well as iron and coal workings in south Wales. Mineral development in

Anglesey and, to a lesser extent, Caernarvonshire owed something to Charles Roe from Macclesfield. The lead mine discovered at Llangynog in north Montgomeryshire in 1692 produced a profit of £140,000 for the Marquess of Powis in 1725–45. Reinvestment of Jamaican money was important in the case of Penrhyn; there was skilful use of local resources by middling gentry elsewhere; and a managerial class was coming to the fore, some of whom, such as Thomas Williams the Copper King, made it into the big time while others, such as William Williams Llandygai, were happy to take subordinate positions. English markets were crucial. Henry Herbert, 1st Earl of Powis of the 2nd creation, benefited in the 1750s and 1760s from demand for Powis oaks for the Royal Navy. Later in the century, Admiral Rodney insisted upon these oaks for his ships, while the extension of the Shropshire Union Canal transported Montgomeryshire timber into the Midlands.

English newspapers circulated in Wales. For example, on 23 May 1761 the *Bristol Chronicle, Or, Universal Mercantile Register*, a weekly launched in January 1760, added named agents in Haverfordwest and Pembroke, and on 20 June 1761 others in Chepstow, Caerleon, Newport, Pontypool, Abergavenny and Raglan. Distribution to Pembrokeshire was presumably by sea, but the expansion into south-east Wales was due to the journeys of a man on horseback, the issue of 20 June noting, 'this paper will, for the future, be constantly vended through . . . Chepstow, Newport, Raglan, Abergavenny, Pontypool and Caerleon, by John Powell . . . [who] will deliver any message or small parcel if properly directed and left at the Printing-Office'. The *Gloucester Journal* of 13 April 1756 named agents in Brecon and Carmarthen. The issue of 16 June 1766 announced 'Advertisements for this paper are taken in by Mr. Morgan Bevan in Swansea, by whom all persons in the counties of Carmarthen, Brecon, and Glamorgan, may be supplied with grocery goods'. In January 1777, the *Bristol Journal* listed named agents in Abergavenny, Brecon, Carmarthen and Haverfordwest. The London press also circulated in Wales. In January 1777, John Campbell wrote from his seat at Stackpole Court in Pembrokeshire to his grandson John, then in London, 'I read in the Publick Advertiser . . . that you had lost at Drury Lane playhouse a fine enamelled gold watch with your crest cypher and motto on the back'.

Communication routes with England did not appreciably improve until the eighteenth century, but this was also true of much of England and Scotland. Between Chester and Hawarden in 1698, Celia Fiennes 'crossed over the marshes, which is hazardous to strangers'. On her return from Wales, she 'forded over the Dee when the tide was out . . . the sands are here soe loose that the tydes does move them . . . many persons that have known the foards well, that have come a year or half a year after, if they venture on their former knowledge have been overwhelm'd in the ditches made by the sands, which is deep enough to swallow up a coach or waggon'.

A century later, travellers were more receptive to the 'picturesque' character of the Welsh landscape, which they constructed in light of the aesthetic preferences of the pre-Romantic movement. This new portrayal of Wales was popularised in a number of works, most prominently, Thomas Pennant's *Tours of Wales* (London, 1778–83) and William Gilpin's *Observations on Several Parts of the Counties of Cambridge . . . Also on Several Parts of North Wales Relative Chiefly to Picturesque Beauty* (London, 1809). Pennant provided pictorial evidence in his *Twelve Views in Aquatint from Drawings taken on the Spot, in South Wales* (London, 1775–7). This view was to be taken up by the Romantics and led to the further dramatisation of Wales.

This was seen for example, in John Martin's painting *The Bard* (1817), which illustrated Thomas Gray's poem of the same name (1757), based on the (subsequently discredited) Welsh tradition mentioned in Thomas Carte's *History of England* (1750) that Edward I ordered the execution of all Welsh bards. Gray had been inspired to complete the poem when he heard a Welsh harpist play at Cambridge. Gray's poem had been the basis of *The Bard*, a painting by Thomas Jones (1743–83), which was the inspiration for later literary and artistic compositions like Martin's. In Martin's painting, the last surviving bard is shown cursing the English troops before plunging to his death. The castle in the background is based on Harlech, but owes more to Alpine views and the dramatic crags round Allendale, which Martin knew from his Northumbrian youth, than to Wales. Gray had written

> On a rock, whose haughty brow
> Frowns o'er old
> Conway's foaming flood,
> Robed in the sable garb of woe,
> With haggard eyes, the Poete stood;
> Loose his beard and hoary hair
> Stream'd like a meteor
> through the troubled air.

Such an account of the Welsh landscape left scant role for people and, indeed, as with the contemporary cult for the English Lake District and the Scottish Highlands, was part of a process by which the character of much of

Britain was separated from its peoples and the rapid socio-economic changes they were experiencing.

Travel in Wales was improved by the spread of turnpike roads, although initially this was very slow. In 1750 there was a turnpike system in England, but not Wales. Thus, at that point, the already bad communication system arising from the limited nature of inland waterways looked as though it would receive no improvement by road. However, Wales benefited from the major expansion in 1750–70, and important routes included Hereford to Brecon (1757) and to Haverfordwest (1787), Newtown to Aberystwyth (1769), and Cardiff to Neath, and on to Carmarthen. Coastal shipping remained crucial for freight, drove roads for animals.

The major developments in eighteenth-century Wales were religious. Evangelicalism was linked to efforts to spread education and reform society. Anglicans and Dissenters waged campaigns against Catholicism, drunkenness and profanity, and for salvation and literacy. These religious moral campaigns were part of a cult of improvements that linked religious revival in the seventeenth century to later interest in secular reform.

The *Gloucester Journal* of 10 April 1780 carried a report from Glamorgan that announced the prizes offered by the Glamorgan Society for the Encouragement of

Agriculture. The item noted the problems facing agricultural improvement:

> The form and situation of this county, as well as the illiterateness of the generality of small farmers make us near a century behind some parts of England in the art of agriculture . . . The gentlemen of this county, from their observations in travelling, and from books, and their own experience, discover many improvements as to mode of tillage, different kinds of manure, succession of crops, artificial grasses, implements, etc. which they cannot prevail upon the farmers to adopt so speedily, any other ways as by pecuniary rewards, and an honorary distinction among the gentlemen will dispose them the more to make experiements, and to instruct and convince their respective tenants and neighbours by the superior force of example.

That year, the Society awarded prizes (among others) for the best crops of cabbages, red clover seed, rye grass seed, potatoes, sainfoin and turnip seed, for reclaiming rough lands, draining land, and being an active Highway Surveyor. The Brecknockshire Society, founded in 1755, sought to achieve similar goals. Visiting his Cardiganshire estate for the first time in 1780, Thomas Johnes was angered by the poor condition of the estate and tenantry.

The timber had been denuded, transport was by ox-sledge, there was little rotation, ploughs were poor and fertilisers primitive. Johnes sought to bring improvement under each of these heads and was a particularly vigorous planter of trees, although he later suffered a financial collapse.

The use of the Welsh language was controversial. Some clerics and squires sought to suppress it, as did the charity schools. The schools founded by the Puritan Thomas Gouge's Welsh Trust in the 1670s used English as the teaching medium and were designed to teach the poor to read English. Gouge founded more than 300 schools and distributed copies of the Bible. The Society for the Propagation of Christian Knowledge followed from 1699, and provided charity schools and copies of the Bible. The Reverend Griffith Jones of Llanddowror (1683–1761) was much abused and denounced as a secret spreader of Methodism because from the 1730s he stressed the need to use Welsh as the medium of a popular literacy campaign and to catechise in it. In 1737 alone, Jones opened 37 schools, and he was partly responsible for the edition of the Bible and Prayer Book in Welsh issued by the Society for Promoting Christian Knowledge in 1746. Griffith Jones encouraged the reading of the Welsh Bible as a way to revive Christian life and teach moral precepts. His educational policy and sense of mission was indeed conducive to the spread of Methodism, which shared a tendency to think in terms of new possibilities and rebirth. Jones was a product of an important current of religious philanthropy that did much to shape the character of modern Wales. He had helped the Society for the Promotion of Christian Knowledge which itself drew on Gouge's Welsh Trust. Both the Society and Jones were greatly helped by the Pembrokeshire landowner Sir John Phillips.

Religious radicalism also flourished. In addition to 'old' Dissent – Baptists and Independents (Congregationalists) – there was now the 'new' Dissent – Wesleyans and Calvinistic Methodists. The Great Revival of the mid-eighteenth century led to the rapid growth of a distinctly Welsh form of Methodism that was centred on Calvinistic theology, represented in England by George Whitfield, a close co-operator with Howell Harris. Inspired by the preaching of the Anglican vicar of Talgarth in 1735, Harris (1714–73) became a formidable itinerant missionary preacher for the revived Christianity that was to become Welsh Methodism. His call for Christian living was not always popular. At the Monmouth races in 1740, Harris attacked 'balls, assemblies, horseraces, whoredom and drunkenness', and provoked a riot.

Methodism was to be the characteristic creed of the Welsh-speaking areas of north and west Wales in the nineteenth century. The first two Methodist chapels in Caernarvonshire were built at Tŷ-mawr in 1752 and in Clynnog in about 1764. There were many others before the end of the century. The Baptists also made a powerful impact in North Wales. Like the Congregationalists and Methodists, they founded chapels and had many cottage meetings. The south Wales valleys were also strongly Nonconformist: acknowledgement of Independent and Presbyterian roots there helps to temper the common idea that the Calvinistic Methodists suddenly conquered the whole country in c. 1800. Nevertheless, the growth of the new Dissent was still slow in the eighteenth century, and only really took off in the nineteenth.

Dissent was not necessarily radical, although the Baptists and Independents were inclined to radicalism. The Act of Toleration of 1689 had eased the position of Nonconformists, although the civil disabilities imposed under the Test Act were not repealed until 1828. This situation encouraged a sense of difference and exclusion without driving it to the point of rebellion or millenarian fervour. Furthermore, in many places, Calvinistic Methodism was actually a Tory connection. Wesleyanism was also very conservative. An equation of Nonconformist with Liberal and radical was arguably only true after 1868.

Socio-religious developments in the eighteenth century – the spread of education, religious revival, and a campaign against illiteracy – were to have a more fundamental impact on the future of Wales and the character of the Welsh than the corrupt political system under the Hanoverians, being central to Welsh historical memory and laying the foundations for the culture of nineteenth-century Wales. The actual 'conquest of the countryside' by the Nonconformists, however, was really in *c.* 1790–1820, beginning a critical stage in the Nonconformist cultural hegemony. Between *c.* 1810 and 1840, this destroyed the traditional culture of Wales: plays, fairs and feasts all falling as this new Welsh Reformation hit hard at everyday life. The new religious current also affected education, leading for example to the opening of numerous Sunday schools. Furthermore, the emergence of radical thought (religious Dissenting activity, often associated with the Unitarians) in the period surrounding the War of American Independence (1775–83) and the French Revolution (1789) was to be the basis of Nonconformist radicalism in the nineteenth century.

FOUR

FROM INDUSTRIAL REVOLUTION TO THE TWENTIETH CENTURY

INDUSTRIALISATION

Religious energy has been a central feature of much modern Welsh history, but so also was another eighteenth-century development: the rise of industry, although, as already indicated, this can be traced back to the sixteenth century and, indeed, longer in the case of coal mining and ironworking. Wales for long had had more to export than livestock. Nevertheless, in the eighteenth century, especially the second half, coal, iron and lead production grew rapidly, helping to turn the interest of many gentry families to industry and mineral exploitation. This in turn transformed Wales from a predominantly rural into a predominantly urban society during the nineteenth century. The Welsh landscape was already changing. In 1776, Jabez Fisher found at Tintern not only the spectacular ruins of the abbey but also a great Manufactury of Wire, the Iron being manufac- tured from the Ore, a furnace to make it into Barrs from whence it is taken to the tilting Mill, where it is lengthened out into long rods. It is then drawn thro the holes of the different sizes till it be reduced to the desired fineness. The whole operation is performed by water by the addition of very little Labor.

Yet, human labour was important in much industry. John 'Warwick' Smith's painting of Mynydd Parys – *Interior of one of the Copper Mines on the Paris Mountain* showed men breaking up the rock and other men turning the wheel to lower baskets into the mine. Jabez Fisher also visited the copper-smelting site at White Rock near Swansea, founded in 1737:

Here are 43 Furnaces constantly in Blast, all employed in their proper departments, and 150 Men who appear like what we might conceive of the Inhabitants of Pandaemonium. The greatest decorum is however preserved; they all move like a Machine.

The availability of coal helped attract copper-smelting to south Wales, but coastal shipping was also important. The copper works in the lower Swansea Valley depended on sea-borne supplies, and used Cornish, Irish and Welsh

(Anglesey) copper. The valley dominated the non-ferrous smelting industry of the world. Economic growth was linked to Britain's wars and the burgeoning demands of its Empire. Metallurgical industries, especially gun founding, developed, and Welsh ironmasters were keen to adopt new technological developments. North-east Wales was important in this sphere.

Wales was also directly involved in the conflict with France (1793–1802, 1803–15) as well as with arms production. The American Col. William Tate's poorly disciplined 1,400 strong *Légion Noire* (named after their dark-brown coats, captured from the British at Quiberon Bay and dyed) landed at Carreg Wastad at Pembrokeshire on 22 February 1797. Once landed, the French seized food and alcohol, while the Fishguard Fencibles, only 190 strong, retreated. However, the defence was rallied by Lord Cawdor, the local aristocrat, who assembled a 600-strong force and advanced with determination. Intimidated by this advance and affected by a collapse of confidence, Tate surrendered on 24 February. The French had planned to win the support of the local poor and disaffected and to press on to attack and burn Bristol. Although the invasion force included two troops of grenadiers, much of it was composed of jail-sweepings and Tate was not up to the task.

There was nothing in Wales to compare with the Irish rising in 1798. Instead, there was much patriotism. Nelson's destruction of the French fleet at the Battle of the Nile in Aboukir Bay in 1798 was celebrated by the construction of the Naval Temple by a local dining club on the Kymin in south Wales. There was widespread support for the Militia and for the Volunteer units. Just under four per cent of the total male population in Wales and Scotland volunteered to join home defence units in 1793–7 as opposed to just over two per cent in England. Welsh willingness was less apparent after war resumed in 1803. There was a clear difference between south Wales, which was far more willing to provide volunteers, than north and central Wales, although Anglesey and Flintshire provided a high percentage of eligible men for the Militia and Volunteers in 1804. Carmarthenshire and Denbighshire were far less enthusiastic. Militia and Volunteer units staged elaborate manoeuvres and were familiarised with military conditions. For example, a mock landing at Swansea on 23 April 1804 was driven back by infantry fire and cavalry. Some of the Welsh aristocracy also played a prominent role in the war. Henry, Lord Paget, later 1st Marquess of Anglesey, lost a leg at Waterloo, and two of his brothers fought in the Napoleonic Wars. He improved his seat at Plas Newydd with the profits from his copper mines. Ordinary soldiers were less fortunate. The Napoleonic Wars also encouraged efforts to increase agricultural production, most prominently by the enclosure of 'waste'.

Growth became more sustained from the 1790s and was also increasingly concentrated in coal and iron-rich south Wales. By 1796, there were 25 furnaces in south Wales, including three at Cyfarthfa (which from 1794 belonged to Richard Crawshay), and three at Dowlais, where development had begun in 1759. In contrast only one furnace had survived in north Wales. By 1811, there were 148 furnaces in south Wales and, due to the use of coke (rather than charcoal) and the steam-engine, their yield increased. In 1810, a furnace at Ynys Fach, near Merthyr, produced what was then the record of 105 tons a week. The production of pig iron in south Wales rose from 5,000 tons in 1720 to 525,000 by 1840: 36 per cent of the British total. The tremendous industrial expansion in Monmouthshire and east Glamorgan, at for example Ebbw Vale and Merthyr Tydfil, created numerous jobs and helped lead to a permanent demographic shift. The largest town in Wales in 1801 was Merthyr Tydfil, no more than a hamlet in 1750, but now the leading centre of the coke and blast-furnace-based iron industry of south Wales and the leading centre of iron production in the world. Glamorgan and Monmouthshire had about 20 per cent of the Welsh population in 1801, 57.5 per cent in 1901 and 60–65 per cent since 1921.

The growth in the south Wales coalfield was also important. Welsh coal was suited for coking for iron furnaces and for steamships, and Welsh anthracite coal was ideal for the hot blast process for the iron and steel industry. Economic growth put pressure on communications, not least because coal and iron were bulk products. The Glamorgan iron-masters encouraged the construction of a road from Cardiff along the Taff Valley, and in 1793–4 of the Glamorgan Canal which provided inexpensive bulk transport. The mountainous terrain, however, meant that most of Wales was particularly badly suited for canal construction. This made the possibility of digging the Glamorgan Canal especially important, but also ensured that the railway would have even more of an impact than it did in the English Midlands. The development of the port of Cardiff by the Marquess of Bute and the spread of the railway, especially the Taff Vale line between Cardiff and Merthyr Tydfil (1841), permitted the movement of large quantities of coal. In the decade after 1856 exports from south Wales led to the opening of three new dock developments, the Bute East, Roath Basin and Penarth docks, all linked to the Taff Vale Railway which brought the coal from the Glamorgan coalfield. Production of coal in millions of tons rose from 1.2 in 1801 to 10.25 by 1860, 13.6 by 1870 and 57 by 1913. Improvements in mine technology, especially in drainage and ventilation, made possible the working of deeper seams and thus a rapid expansion of the coalfield and a rise in production. The major area of mining in the eighteenth century had been in the Neath and Swansea area, but in the early nineteenth century there was major expansion in the copper valleys of the Rivers Taff and Cynon, and from the 1860s in the Rhondda Valley and the eastern section. Not only was more coal dug in south Wales, but its importance in the national output rose: from about 2.7 per cent in 1750 to 15 per cent in the 1830s, 17.08 per cent in the 1890s, and 19 per cent in 1900–13, the last a percentage reduced by the 1910–11 mine strike.

North Wales was far less important. The coalfield there (in north-east Wales) never saw the same production figures. Instead, its output never surpassed five million tons per annum and at its maximum importance – the 1850s – it was producing about 2.05 per cent of British production.

Most of the Welsh coal was exported and the coal industry employed about a third of the Welsh male labour force. Coal furthered industrialisation, especially the emergence of Cardiff as the Welsh metropolis: its population rose from fewer than 2,000 in 1801 and 10,000 in 1841, to 200,000 in 1921; that of the coal mining Rhondda from under 1,000 in 1851 to 153,000 in 1911.

The presence of coal encouraged the development of metallurgical industries. Founded by John Vivian from Truro in 1809, the Hafod works in the lower Swansea valley were developed under the management of his son John Henry Vivian into one of the largest and most up-to-date metallurgical enterprises in Europe. Copper smelting was the core of the Vivian business but, by the mid-1870s, they also ran nickel, cobalt, silver, alkali and phosphate works, collieries and an iron foundry. North-east Wales was also a region of significant economic growth, in which coal and metallurgical enterprises played major roles near Wrexham. Like Swansea, Flint was a centre for alkali manufacture, an important early stage in the chemical industry. The presence of coal was important, but so also was Cheshire salt and north Wales limestone. Other chemical plants in the 1880s were found near Cardiff and on Anglesey.

Economic growth changed the rest of the economy. New markets were created for Welsh agriculture. Communications greatly improved in the nineteenth century. The Conwy Suspension Bridge, built by Thomas Telford and completed in 1826, replaced the ferry that had previously been the sole way to cross the river. William Jones's travel letters from 1775 indeed recorded numerous ferries. Telford's bridge was part of an improvement to road transport that in sum helped open up north Wales, ensuring that Holyhead became a more important port for Dublin. The opening of the Menai Suspension Bridge in 1826 helped lead to the ending of ferries across the Menai Straits at Porthaethwy (1826), Beaumaris (1830), and Abermenai (1840s). There were also improvements to open up the slate-mining district, especially in the 1820s. In the early 1840s, a regular coach service was established from Caernarfon to Harlech.

The steam locomotive was to interrupt this development. In 1804, Roger Hopkins built a tramroad between Pen-y-Darren and Abercynon upon which Richard Trevithick tried the first steam railway locomotive engine. However, Trevithick's locomotive was built for a bet, and had no real impact. Locomotive technology achieved a breakthrough in the 1820s, although with no immediate impact in Wales, and in the 1830s bold trunk schemes were advanced and started. With the development of wrought-iron rails in the 1820s and 1830s (the rails themselves were at least as important as the locomotives), rail began to take over from road through-out Britain. The Chester and Holyhead Railway was incorporated in 1844 with a capital of £2,100,000 and the line opened from Chester to Bangor in 1848. The Menai Straits were bridged by the Britannia Tubular Bridge in 1850 and the journey time from London to Holyhead cut to 9 hours 35 minutes, compared to 40 hours by mail coach. The South Wales Railway from Cardiff reached Neath in 1850, Carmarthen in 1852 and Haverfordwest in 1854. Newport and Gloucester were linked in 1851, and the line from Merthyr reached Brecon in 1862. The Manchester and Milford Haven Railway was planned in 1845 to give Manchester access to other ports so that it could compete with Liverpool. The route went via Shrewsbury, Aberystwyth and Cardigan. The railway reached Aberystwyth in 1864. By 1867 the whole route was connected for through traffic.

Use of the railway overcame many of the limitations of earlier transport systems and encouraged economic development. Rail links were therefore also crucial to the communities that grew up to serve the new concerns. Railways, for example, helped speed north Wales slates toward urban markets. The Ffestiniog Railway of 1836 linked the slate mines with Porthmadog harbour, the Padarn Railway line of 1843 doing the same for

Dinorwig quarry and Port Dinorwic; and the rail network in the area improved from 1867, when a line was opened between Caernarfon and Porthmadog via Afon-wen. Railways spread elsewhere. For example, the Anglesey Central Railway, authorised by Parliament in 1863, was completed to Amlwich in 1867 with a branch line from Pentreberw to Red Wharf Bay opened in 1909. There were still many areas, however, that were not served, and thus the railway encouraged the development of feeder carriage and cart services.

Steam also had an impact at sea. Steamships put pressure on less expensive but less reliable and slower sailing ships, and harbours were built or improved to benefit from steamships, Porthmadog harbour being opened in 1824 to export slates, and Port Dinorwic enlarged in 1829 for the same purpose, although Porthmadog long remained a stronghold of sail.

Coach services, droving and coastal shipping declined with the spread of rail. The railway also hit river traffic, which was generally very important in north Wales from medieval times to the 1870s. The opening of the railway to Barmouth in 1867 wrecked the lighterage carriage up-river to Dolgellau. In 1866, 167 ships entered and left the port, but only eleven in 1876. Nevertheless, coastal shipping remained important until 1914 in some places.

Commercial sail lingered on until the Second World War, or even later.

The spread of the rail system created fresh demand for iron. William Crawshay (1788–1867), who succeeded his grandfather Richard as the proprietor of the Cyfarthfa Ironworks, increased the number of furnaces there in the 1850s and 1860s from six to eleven and nearly doubled their average yield. The autocratic nature of Crawshay's sway was captured in the complacent biography by George Clement Boase published in the *Dictionary of National Biography*: 'His will was law: in his home and business he tolerated no opposition. With his workmen he was strictly just.' For his successor as manager, his youngest son, Robert Crawshay (1817–79), the account was even more complacent and misleading: 'upwards of five thousand men, women and children employed at Cyfarthfa, all receiving good wages, and well looked after by their master . . . averse to unions . . . called his men together and warned them of the consequences of persisting in their unreasonable demands; but as they would not yield the furnaces were one by one put out'.

SOCIAL CHANGE AND PRESSURES

Economic growth in the industrial regions led to a decline in the relative importance of agriculture and rural Wales, and to a reorientation in the standard images of Welsh-ness, although the evangelical movement of the nineteenth century and in particular the rise of Nonconformity were also important in the new perception of national character and interest. Anglicans became outnumbered and the growth of Dissent played a major role in reshaping Wales politically: the religious census of 1851 revealed that over 80 per cent of worshippers were Nonconformists. In place of the dominance of conservative Anglican gentry, the Liberal party, based on Dissent, was dominant from 1868 to 1918. Of the twenty-eight Liberal MPs elected in 1880, eight were Nonconformists. A Nonconformist religious revival in the early 1900s that was politically charged by opposition to the Conservative government's policy on church schools helped sweep the Liberals to a record victory in Wales in the 1906 election. The Nonconformist press played a significant role in the growth of radical Nonconformity, and the political and cultural affiliations of Nonconformity were also important in the growth of national feeling. The continued existence of Anglican privileges in a predominantly Nonconformist country became the burning issue in nineteenth-century Wales, and the eradication of Anglican privilege in a largely Nonconformist country shaped the character of Welsh nationalism. Nonconformity placed a great emphasis on reading and preaching, and fostered a very self-conscious and self-confident culture. Nonconformist clergy were largely drawn from the masses.

The nineteenth-century transformation of Wales was sweeping. Industrialisation was not achieved without traumatic change, and the work that was required of people was back-breaking, dangerous and alienating. After the widespread corn riots of the 1790s, there were waves of riots in the industrial areas of Wales in the first three decades of the nineteenth century. The south Wales coal and iron district was generally unsettled in these years. The government was worried, and the image of Wales in the first half of the century is one of considerable resort to force. Wales was seen by government as an area potentially out of control, which helps explain government interest, in the form of official reports, and their tone. The image of Wales projected in the report of the education commissioners in 1847 – Wales as a land of theft, perjury and immorality – seems to confirm this. In their report, the so-called 'Treason of the Blue Books', the commissioners had attributed the shortcomings of the Welsh to their language. This image accounts for so much Welsh middle-class striving for respectability, and an image of respectability, in the second half of the century.

Merthyr Tydfil, the centre of early industrialisation, had a full range of industrial disputes in the early decades of the century, with violent riots against the 'Iron Kings' in 1800 and particular bitterness in 1831. The Merthyr Rising collapsed in the face of military action and its own divisions, but at least twenty rioters were killed. Eight years later, on 3 November 1839, a Chartist rising of over 5,000 men, in which many colliers, under John Frost, sought to seize Newport, as part of a revolutionary uprising, was stopped when a small group of soldiers opened fire and the rioters dispersed. Frost was arrested. The same year, the Rebecca Riots began in south-west Wales: attacks on the tollgates that handicapped the rural economy. The riots persisted until 1844 and extended their targets to include attacks on unfair rents and workhouses. 'Mother Rebecca', the symbolic leader of the protests, with a white gown and red or black face, was named from the Rebecca of *Genesis* 'possessing the gates of them which hate thee'. The 293 crowd attacks on tollgates in 1839–44 reflected considerable social alienation, the product of the industrial depression of 1839–42, of the inflation of land rents during the Napoleonic War, and of hostility to landlords, Church tithes and the loss of common land through the widespread enclosures of 1750–1815, as well as to the high charges of the turnpike trusts. Hostility was also expressed by poaching and arson. Earlier, imposition of enclosures had led to disturbances, as in Caernarvonshire in 1809, 1810 and 1812. The loss of traditional rights greatly affected the livelihood of the poor and was also seen as an abuse of power.

The response of the authorities was to deploy the coercive power of the state: in Caernarvonshire, troops were used against enclosure rioters, the Riot Act was read, and rioters were imprisoned and, on occasion, transported. Most major landlords were unpopular as Tories, but conservative interests remained strong in some rural areas. Thus, Henry, heir to the Duchy of Beaufort, a solid Tory, was MP for Monmouth in 1813–32, and his brother Granville was MP for the county from 1828–48 and another firm Tory. The vicious mantraps displayed on the Ballroom Staircase at Powis Castle are a reminder of the harsh war fought with poachers and the extent to which deference was limited.

The Rebecca disturbances faded after an Act of 1844 replaced turnpike trusts with highway boards in south Wales, but the following decades saw a series of serious coal strikes in Glamorgan. Nevertheless, it is necessary to put this militancy in context. Strikes were a natural response to a poorly-regulated industry, and in the south Wales coalfield many were specific to particular pits: worker unity was limited, and trade union organisation poor. Glamorgan was affected by the wave of strikes linked to Chartism that have been termed the General Strike of 1842, but it was the only Welsh county to be so, and Glamorganshire was far less disturbed than Lancashire or the Potteries.

What is more obvious is that the revolutionary sentiment that did exist did not lead to a full-blown revolution. The process of transformation from without, largely by wealthy English people, especially Bristol and London financiers, took place without the Welsh doing much to resist. The first newspapers in Wales – Swansea's *The Cambrian* in 1804 and Bangor's *North Wales Chronicle* in 1808 – did not issue clarion calls for autonomy.

There was nothing to compare with the Year of Revolutions (1848) on the Continent. Troops from the garrison at Brecon did play an important role in a number of disputes, but the number of regulars in south Wales in 1839 was only raised to 1,000, although the authorities were vigilant for many years and had plans to deploy troops rapidly from nearby English and Irish counties. Nevertheless, this scarcely compared with

Habsburg forces in Hungary and Italy. Furthermore, Wales provided troops for the army. In addition, some of the leaders of the British military came from Wales: the 1st Lord Raglan, who had been one of Wellington's officers in the Peninsular War, was Commander-in-Chief in the Crimea in 1854–5.

The British empire and the wider world also provided many opportunities for those who were less well-connected, such as the explorer Henry Morton Stanley, born John Rowlands in Denbigh in 1841 in dubious circumstances. The wider world also provided opportunities for those Welsh men and women who decided to leave their native country for pastures new. Both Canada and the USA were to have thriving Welsh emigrant communities. Michael D. Jones, a committed nationalist, undertook an ill-fated attempt to establish a Welsh community in Patagonia in 1865: this proved more difficult than expected and did not fulfil the hopes of the people involved.

Far from south Wales being 'held down', revolutionary sentiment was limited, while most industrial disputes were restricted to specific grievances. There was only a limited sense of worker solidarity and it was unusual for agitation to be far-flung. Trade unionism emerged only slowly, as employers resisted attempts at workers' organisation. Migration to developing industrial regions eased rural poverty.

Political pressures, however, are not only expressed through violence. The new socio-economic order created through industrialisation was one that sat ill with traditional hierarchies, allegiances and practices. This was true both of emerging working-class consciousness and of those who ran the new world of industry. If this subverted secular and ecclesiastical hierarchies, it also challenged assumptions of Welshness, although these were of course already contingent. In part this was due to immigration. Industrialisation brought great demands for labour, particularly in the coalfields and iron works of south and north-east Wales, and this was exacerbated as coal mining expanded greatly in south Wales from the 1850s on. Initially, most of the necessary labour came from rural Wales, although an appreciable Irish contingent also settled in Merthyr Tydfil. There was far less Irish immigration to north Wales. The Irish immigration also affected Swansea and Cardiff in a big way after the initial impact on Merthyr. Alongside subsequent immigration, this was largely responsible for the Catholic Church being one of the major religious bodies in twentieth-century Wales.

From the 1850s, large numbers of English immigrants settled in south Wales. In 1861, 11 per cent of Swansea's population had been born in south-west England. Wales was unusual in Europe in having a net immigration rate in the nineteenth century, although there was Welsh emigration, both overseas and to England, especially to the nearby counties of Lancashire, Cheshire, Shropshire and Herefordshire. The immigrants had no commitment to Welsh culture which was anyway in a state of flux in the rapidly industrialising regions. English immigrants jumped into the melting pot, just like the people from the rural hinterland. The ascendancy of Nonconformity was threatened by the influx of English Anglicans and, to a lesser extent, Irish Catholics. As a result, the Welsh language which had been the centre of debate in the 1840s, not least with the publication of the controversial Blue Books on Education in 1847, came to be of far less consequence in the areas of Wales that were increasingly the centres of economic power and political represent- ation, although over half the population of Wales still spoke Welsh in 1901. Furthermore, despite the immigra- tion, the industrial towns like Merthyr and Swansea were major centres for Welsh culture throughout the nineteenth century. There was also an enormous Welsh- language press.

Nevertheless, English immigration and the use of English helped to make south Wales seem alien to the north Welsh. When, in 1895–6, David Lloyd George campaigned in south Wales in pursuit of his attempt to merge the Liberal Federations in north and south Wales, he complained privately that the people were 'semi-English' or 'Newport Englishmen' buried in 'morbid footballism'. In turn, the meeting of the South Wales Liberal Federation at Newport in January 1896 rejected his attempt to create a single Welsh Liberal organisation. Lloyd George was never to be particularly popular in south Wales. Cultural nationalism proved to be a more potent force than political nationalism, which only succeeded in exposing the differences which existed in Wales.

It was not only thanks to immigration, however, that the Welsh language became less widely used. The use of English was also encouraged throughout Wales by members of the emerging middle class. Gentry landowners were commonly English-speaking, but they had less of a linguistic impact than groups that were becoming more important as the economy of all of Wales was affected by economic growth and integration: cattle dealers, merchants, shopkeepers, master mariners. English was the language of commerce, the language in which financial records were kept, and the language of education. Hostile attitudes to the Welsh language by officialdom and by the gentry and middle classes of Wales were reflected in the controversial education reports, the Blue Books of 1847. Nevertheless, the absolute numbers of Welsh-speakers grew in the nineteenth century, and, then and for a long time afterwards, many areas were still effectively monoglot. Welsh was too much the language of religion, and was deemed to be flourishing when religion was flourishing. Welsh was central to Sunday school and was increasingly accepted in schools from the late nineteenth century.

Economic growth brought change in many spheres and much disruption. The accompanying tensions were experienced not only by social groups but also by communities, families and individuals. There was much uncertainty, a situation that encouraged resort to religion and/or drink. Thus, for example, the papers of solicitors from the period reveal the extent to which debt was a problem at every social level, from great houses such as Nanteos in Cardiganshire to the families of lead and slate miners dependent on the expedients of the poor.

THE RISE OF LIBERAL WALES

As the use of English became more common, it also became more politically charged, a consequence in part of debates over the role and nature of public education.

Furthermore, in the second half of the nineteenth century, language came to play a role in a powerful political critique directed against Conservative landowners and the Anglican Church and in favour of Liberalism and Nonconformity, both of which were presented as truly Welsh. Thus T.E. (Thomas) Ellis, elected as Liberal MP for Merioneth in 1886, declared in his election address his support for Home Rule for Ireland and Wales, the disestablishment of the Church of England in Wales, a revision of the Land Laws, and better educational facilities that were under the control of public, not Anglican, bodies. Welsh played a role in many of the schools established under the Welsh Intermediate and Technical Education Act of 1889, a state education system different to that in England. Earlier, English had dominated schools, and indeed been compulsory in the Board Schools established under the 1870 Education Act.

There was also a greater interest in Welsh cultural history and identity, a growth in Welsh poetry, the development of choral singing and the 'revival' of the national eisteddfod. This represented a success for the revival of the bardic craft by Edward Williams, Iolo Morganwg (1747–1826), a stonemason, shopkeeper, forger of ancient manuscripts, charlatan, genius and poet, akin to a William Blake on opium. Iolo concocted much of the basis of the modern eisteddfod movement, including druidical ceremonies, but his successful attempt at inventing tradition played an important role in giving the Welsh people a sense of their own national distinctiveness. Ironically, it was due to the patronage of the wealthy, Anglicised landlords that the eisteddfod developed as an institution between 1815 and 1860. There were also altogether starchier (and far more influential) later nineteenth-century exponents of Welshness, such as Sir Owen Edwards and Sir John Morris Jones. Publishing in Welsh increased: for example, on Anglesey, the press of Lewis Jones at Holyhead produced *Llais y Wlad*, the first Anglesey newspaper, while David Jones at Amlwch and another Lewis Jones at Llannerch-y-medd also published extensively in Welsh. The Welsh national anthem was composed in 1856.

A range of new institutions, from University College Aberystwyth (opened in 1872), testified to a stronger sense of national identity, the institutionalisation of which created bodies that had an interest in its furtherance and that provided a vital platform and focus for those seeking to assert Welsh identities. University Colleges were also founded at Cardiff (1883) and Bangor (1884). The University of Wales, encompassing these three colleges, was given its Royal Charter in 1893. Swansea became the fourth constituent college of the federal University of Wales in 1920. The first university college in Wales, Lampeter, had been founded by the Bishop of St Davids as a Church institution in 1822 (it opened in 1827). Both the National Library and the National Museum were authorised by royal charter in 1907; the Library opened in 1909, the Museum was begun in 1910 but not opened until 1920. This was a period of great excitement, optimism and activity. There was a heady mix of religious and political radicalism, an intensely literate and self-confident culture, and a booming imperial economy. The great preachers also played a vital role as 'tribunes of the people'.

In political terms, the assertion of Welsh identities was largely represented by Liberalism which increasingly swept Wales: all five of the Glamorgan constituencies were Liberal from 1857, 19 of the 30 Welsh seats (excluding Monmouthshire) after the 1874 election and 28 of the 30 seats after the 1880 election. Married to a Welsh woman, the Liberal leader William Gladstone himself lived in Wales in Hawarden from 1839 to his death in 1898. Henry Richard won at Merthyr Tydfil in 1868 on a vibrantly nationalist platform in which Liberalism, Nonconformity and the 'Welsh nation' were fused. Landlord/landed gentry political control had collapsed. This reflected the extension of the franchise thanks to the 1867 and 1884 Reform Acts, but even more the secret ballot, and was the product of a clash of class, religion, culture and language. Conservative control was swept away in 1880, although there had been important moves in this direction in 1868 and 1874. The 1884 Act was followed by a redistribution of constituencies that brought more seats to areas such as Glamorgan. The 1884 Act and the redistribution of seats transformed the balance of power in rural areas. In 1906, not one Conservative was returned for Wales's 30 Westminster seats. Aside from Keir Hardie at Merthyr, all fell to the Liberals, who seemed to be set fair to contain the threat which the infant Labour Party posed to their Welsh ascendancy. Indeed, Hardie came second to Liberal candidates at Merthyr (a double-member constituency) in the four elections held between 1900 and 1910.

The benefits of economic growth were spread very unequally. At one extreme, owners reaped great benefit, and spent it. Aside from the splendid houses of the period, there was also an upsurge in the creation of gardens, as with the gardens at Duffryn set up by Thomas Mawson for the Cardiff shipowner, Reginald Cory, from 1906. Life for most, however, was far bleaker.

Furthermore, growth in some industries had been succeeded by serious problems. This was particularly true of the iron industry. That was hit by the exhaustion of easily worked deposits of iron ore, which necessitated more difficult deeper workings, and competition from more easily worked English and foreign deposits. Furthermore, the invention of the Bessemer steel-making process and the Siemens' open-hearth furnace posed serious problems of obsolescence, leading to the need for expensive investment. Many furnaces were shut and there was much disruption and hardship in the 1870s and 1880s.

More generally, Wales did not benefit as much from the new industries of the late nineteenth century as it did from the earlier focus on coal and iron. Thus, chemicals, electrical industries and, later, the early stages of the car industry did not develop strongly in Wales. There were no motor car manufacturers there in 1913, when such production was widely-dispersed. Nor were there any manufacturers of electrical cables, dynamos, motors or transformers in Wales in 1910. The lack of alternative industries to coal and iron served to exacerbate the economic problems which Wales was later to experience.

This was more, however, than a failure to develop a second stage. From the outset, the industrial revolution in Wales had been limited in scope, focused in particular on coal and iron and without the development in heavy engineering, shipbuilding and locomotive manufacture seen in north-east England or of textiles seen in Lancashire and Yorkshire. As a result, job opportunities for women were relatively limited, especially in south Wales, thus putting further pressure on wages from mining and heavy industry. There were locomotive works in Cardiff, Llanidloes, and Ruabon, but the major works were elsewhere: the Great Western Railway workshops were in Swindon and Wolverhampton, the London and North Western Railway workshops in Crewe and Wolverton, not Wales. There were boilermakers in south Wales, but Wales was not the major centre of steam-engine manufacture. Nor was it important in agricultural engineering, still less textile machinery.

As with many other what ifs, it is difficult to assess the likely impact of a wider initial industrial base and/or of significant non-coal based developments in the closing decades of the century. They certainly would have tempered the dominance of coal and might have lessened the development of industrial militancy in the late Edwardian period. They would also have prevented the Welsh economy from descending into deep depression in the inter-war period. Furthermore, the industrial impact was cumulative: a lack of engineering skills lessened the probability of new industries, such as the aero-industry, developing or locating in Wales.

Meanwhile, rural Wales had changed. In 1868, there was clear social tension in the election for the Caernarvonshire county seat. The wealthy Vaynol Estate under the Assheton-Smiths backed the Conservative candidate, as did the other landed families, but the Liberal landlord, Love Jones Parry, was elected. Tenants and quarrymen had defied landlords and employers. The Vaynol Estate increased its unpopularity by evicting John Owen of Tŷn-Llwyn, a supporter of Parry who had been threatened with eviction if he would not toe the line. There were many other evictions as well. In 1885, Sir Watkin Williams Wynn was defeated in east Denbighshire, but evictions did not follow there.

The position of landlords was also hit by the severe agrarian depression of the last quarter of the century, as cheap imports of food from North America, Australasia and Argentina brought by steamships depressed prices. North American grain encouraged a move away from grain, throughout Wales, especially in south Wales; but beef, mutton and lamb sales were affected by the introduction of refrigerated holds, which made meat imports from Australia and Argentina possible, and much of Wales, especially west Wales, was not suitable, for reasons of terrain and due to distance from the cities, for milk production. Within Wales, the growth in the milking herd was strongest in Glamorgan and Flintshire, both close to urban markets.

Wales was less badly hit than England or Scotland by agrarian change, in part because it was less reliant on cereals and there was a keen competition for farms. Changes in Schedule B assessments for income tax indicate rent rises in west Wales, but the situation was less favourable further east, especially in Monmouthshire. Rent arrears rose, rebates had to be granted, rent increases were not possible, and the self-confidence of the landed order fell. The rural population was more generally hit, and there was considerable migration from rural areas to industrial regions. This was of such a scale as to cause depopulation – in Anglesey, for example, from 57,000 in 1851 to 49,000 in 1931. Furthermore, local market towns and agricultural processing were hit. The political position of landlords was greatly lessened by the Local Government Act of 1888. This replaced the traditional system of local government, which had been dominated by Justices of the Peace, by elected County Councils. The 1894 Local Government Act added a system of elected councils for towns and rural districts.

These acts amounted to a revolution in local government, which completely destroyed the socio-political power of the gentry.

The sense of change was strengthened by the youth of some of the Liberals, such as Tom Ellis, MP for Merioneth at 27, and David Lloyd George who won Caernarfon Boroughs in 1890 also at 27. Lloyd George's election symbolised the social revolution of the period. A solicitor from modest background, Lloyd George defeated the Conservative candidate, H.J.E. Nanney, who was the squire of Llanystumdwy. He was keen to present this a victory for new Wales and democracy. Lloyd George's background was as a populist. In 1888, he had won much publicity when he fought the Llanfrothen burial case, arguing the right of a quarryman to be buried with Nonconformist rites in an Anglican churchyard in accordance with the Burial Act of 1880. Once elected, Lloyd George criticised the privileges of the aristocracy, landowners, and royalty, although he was far less critical of manufacturing wealth.

As so often with hegemonic concepts, the notion of Liberal Wales is in part misleading. Between 1880 and 1920, the Liberals commonly took only 45–55 per cent of Welsh votes, with 30–35 per cent backing the Conservatives, especially near the English border, in the Vale of Glamorgan, and in Pembrokeshire; as the electorate was expanding (doubling to 127,000 as a result of the 1867 Reform Act and rising to 1.17 million by 1918) this meant that Conservative support was rising substantially in the Anglicised south and east. Presumably many voters were unimpressed by the often tendentious oratory of the Liberals, and, from the 1900s, there was rising support for Labour. Anglicans still tended to vote Conservative. Yet the rise in Conservative support was less than for their opponents.

Similarly, although the religious census in 1851 revealed that Sunday church attendance in Wales was higher than in most of England, especially in Cardigan, Caernarvon, Merioneth and Carmarthen, the rate elsewhere was lower, lowest in Radnor, where half of the population attended no place of worship. Radnor was also the county where the Church of England, later called the Church of Wales, was strongest; it was weakest in the south and in Gwynedd. The Nonconformists – Calvinistic Methodists, Baptists and Congregationalists – were in the majority in all counties bar Radnor, and were especially strong in Merioneth. The Anglican Church nevertheless fought a strong rearguard action in the late nineteenth century. Its revival, and the concurrent decline in Nonconformity, made the issue of disestablishment all the more contentious.

Petitions signed by 267,000 Welsh people led to the Sunday Closing Act for public houses in Wales that was passed in 1881 with the support of 28 Welsh MPs; many, of course, did not sign. The Act, the first since the 1650s to introduce different regulations in Wales, was nevertheless a testimony to the self-righteous determination of Welsh Nonconformity. The Act marked the beginning of English recognition of the need to treat Wales as a Nonconformist rather than an Anglican country. It acted as a symbolic marker of the national distinctiveness of Wales within the United Kingdom. Extended in 1921 to Monmouthshire, the 1881 Act was qualified in 1961 when a new act allowed counties to vote whether they were to become wet or dry. The wet area was extended in each subsequent poll.

Liberalism also drew on concern with social issues and the condition of the people. Industrialisation had produced major strains, and was indeed fatal in many cases. Average life expectancy at birth was higher in rural south-west Wales (over 45) than in industrial and mining south-east Wales (under 45). Ffestiniog slateminers had a particularly high death-rate from fatal accidents: 3.23 per 1,000 workers per year in 1875–93, and that despite the inclusion of slate-mining in the Metaliferous Mines Acts of 1872 and 1875 which sought better working conditions by, for example, improving ventilation. Coal mining was also extremely dangerous, and it remained so. The problems of gas, ventilation and rock-falls claimed many lives. Over 15,000 men died from colliery accidents in the south Wales coalfield in 1910-13, including 439 on one day at the Senghenydd colliery in 1913.

Living conditions were frequently bleak. Much housing was crowded and insanitary, there was much pollution, and it took time to provide clean water. There was improvement, but it took time and action. The infant and early childhood mortality rates remained far higher in south-east than central Wales: indeed the infant rate deteriorated markedly in south Wales between 1841 and 1901. This was especially true of the coalfield and remained the case well into the twentieth century. Lung and respiratory diseases were particularly important in early childhood both there and in the north-east Wales coalfield. Maternal mortality, in contrast, did not correlate to coalfields: it was, for example, very high in parts of Gwynedd. There were improvements: the average death-rate per thousand from typhoid in Ffestiniog fell from 12.9 in 1865–74 to 1.3 in 1880–90, thanks to piped water and a better sewerage system. Nevertheless, the situation remained bleak. The records of Welsh troops discharged on medical grounds in the First World War (1914–18) indicated the strains of pre-war work: Welsh colliers were found to be suffering from hernias and poorly-mended broken bones. The average height of Welsh soldiers was five feet six inches. The harsh conditions of life and work had an impact for decades thereafter: malnourishment in infancy and childhood had a serious effect on health and development.

The education system proved a focus of social concern and control. There was a persistent ideological struggle over elementary education. Anglican 'National Schools' were supported by Anglican landowners and the established Church, but their sectarian purpose was opposed by Nonconformists who, instead, strongly supported 'British' schools from the 1830s. These, however, did not win the support of the landowners. The two systems competed, raising social tension and providing a focus for political division. The middle class tended to use private schools and many were opposed to paying rates to support state schools. Thus the provisions of the 1870 Education Act for the creation of School Boards able to set rates to support non-denominational Board Schools met with widespread opposition, not least from Anglicans concerned to protect their Voluntary Schools and farmers, most of whom were Nonconformists, anxious to retain cheap child labour. Most Nonconformists, in contrast, welcomed the opportunity, but were dismayed by the Act's limitations. Under the 1870 Act, attendance was compulsory between the ages of five and thirteen, and fees were swiftly abolished.

With David Lloyd George, Chancellor of the Exchequer 1908–15 and Prime Minister 1916–22, Welsh Liberalism reached the apex of political power but, as with Ramsay MacDonald and Labour, this was as part of a British political consciousness; and, for Lloyd George, of assimilation into the British governing hierarchy. At the same time, there was a potentially uneasy relationship with the rise of cultural and political nationalism, although the key Welsh issues of the late nineteenth century – land, disestablishment of the Church of England in Wales, and education – could be presented in radical Liberal terms and thus incorporated in British politics. In Wales radical Liberals espoused national issues, particularly disestablishment, hostility to tithes, land reform and public education. Agitation over rents and tithes led to riots, particularly in the Vale of Clwyd in 1887, but landlords were not shot: the Welsh wished to differentiate themselves from the more bitter contemporary agitation in Ireland. The normal Welsh reaction to oppressive landlordism was poaching, not murder. An ethic of non-violence was very important. In addition, opposition focused more on tithes than rents, and was directed against Church representatives, rather than landlords.

Bitter political disputes over disestablishment (first debated in the Commons in 1870), in 1909–13, led to the passage of an Act in 1914, although, due to the war, it was not implemented until 1920, when it was no longer a burning issue. Unlike in Ireland, however, disestablishment was not an adjunct to demands for separatism but, instead, part of the prevailing desire in Wales for English recognition of the distinctive features of Welsh society. The *Cymru Fydd* ('Wales that is to be' or 'Young Wales') Home Rule movement, launched in 1886, was for a time very influential, but foundered in 1895–6 on the antagonism between the north and south Welsh, symbolised by David Lloyd George and D.A. Thomas respectively. The movement was indeed compromised by Lloyd George's ambition as he began to establish himself at Westminster.

It was not surprising that the Welsh Liberals were bitterly opposed to Church schools, especially to measures to provide public assistance to them. The 1902 Balfour Act providing for finance from the rates, passed by a Conservative government, led to non-compliance termed the 'Welsh Revolt', with county councils refusing to implement the Act. This was part of a period of alienation also seen in Welsh hostility to the Boer War of 1899–1902. The Liberals in 1904 won control of every Welsh county council. This led the Conservative government to pass the Education (Local Authorities Default) Act, transferring the operation of the Act to the Board of Education so that support grants in lieu of rates were paid directly to Church schools. This unpopular measure helped the Welsh Liberals to triumph in the 1906 elections. Religion was a crucial aspect of identity and passion, most obviously with the widespread religious revival of 1904–6, a revival that encouraged a sense of the possibility of change that was taken up by many radical workers.

The Nonconformist chapel remained at the centre of community life in late nineteenth-century Wales, but the chapel culture associated with organised Nonconformity began to decline in the last two decades of the nine-teenth century. In the 1880s and 1890s, much of the Welsh working class embraced trade unionism, partic-ularly in the mining valleys of south Wales. Noncon-formity, with its emphasis upon a rural world that was becoming less prominent and the after-life yet to come, had relatively little to offer Welsh workers and colliers.

The trade union lodge displaced the chapel as the main meeting place in the community; chapels came to exist as mere places of worship.

FIVE

THE TWENTIETH CENTURY

Liberalism was to be challenged by the rise of Labour. That reflected the growth of trade unionism from the 1870s and particularly the 1890s. Major strikes in south Wales in 1873–5 hit the iron industry. Bitter disputes over harsh terms of employment wracked the major north Wales slate quarry at Cae Braich y Cafu (generally named Penrhyn after its owner's title of nobility) in 1900–3 and the south Wales coalfield in 1893 and 1898, the last a six-month stoppage, and these helped to radicalise the workforce. The Penrhyn strike was a *cause célèbre* that exposed fissures in Welsh society. The Penrhyn slate quarry was the largest 'hand-made' hole in the earth's surface, and the leading producer of slate in the world throughout the nineteenth century. Production rose from 2,000 tons in 1782 to 130,017 in 1862, as demand rose following the repeal of the slate duty in 1831. The workforce rose from 1,000 in 1820 to 3,000 in 1893, despite the greater use of machinery from the 1850s. The profits were vast. The net annual income in 1859 was £100,000. In the 1820s the profits paid for Penrhyn Castle, a masterpiece of Norman revival architecture, now in the care of the National Trust. Much was also spent on roads, schools, houses and churches on the Caernarvonshire estate of Lord Penrhyn, which by 1893 comprised 72,000 acres, as well as on the contents of the house, not least a major collection of paintings.

The family were paternalistic employers, although this did not ease the respiratory problems produced by slate dust and the effects of silicosis which was not really recognised as an industrial disease at that time. Management was the key issue. The family were strongly opposed to trade unionism. In 1865, the 1st Lord Penrhyn had a recently-formed union of quarrymen dissolved. In 1874, however, a strike led to the recognition in the quarry of the newly-formed North Wales Quarrymen's Union. There were also strikes in Dinorwig quarry in 1874 and 1885–6. Union recognition at Penrhyn was withdrawn by the Conservative 2nd Lord Penrhyn in 1889, but paternalism failed to hold industrial tension at bay. A major strike at Penrhyn in 1896–7 led to an angry debate in the House of Commons, but ended without major concessions from Lord Penrhyn. Similarly, a strike in the slate mines at Llechwedd in 1893 failed. Industrial relations at Penrhyn collapsed again in 1900. A riot against the employment of individual contractors led to the conviction and dismissal of six workers and a strike by the entire workforce. Union recognition became the crucial issue, and the strike attracted national press and political attention. Lloyd George was a bitter critic of Lord Penrhyn. In June 1901, the quarry reopened, but the majority of strikers refused to return to work. Violence by strikers exacerbated the dispute. Eventually the press and the Trades Union Congress ceased their support, and the strike ended in November 1903. This coincided with a slump in the building industry and a fall in production at the quarry.

Meanwhile, in 1901, the Taff Vale case had led to a judgment opening unions to litigation by employers for damages caused by strikes, a major threat to collective bargaining. Class consciousness was rising in the coal industry, helping to strain the Liberal tradition. William Abraham, 'Mabon', the Secretary of the Cambrian Miners' Association and from 1898 President of the new South Wales Miners' Federation, had sought in the 1880s and 1890s to find compromises, and to advance miners' interests without challenging the social order. This mindset was undermined by intransigent pitowners, who were responsible for the 1898 lock-out, and by growing working-class militancy. 'Mabon' had had little time for strikes, but his successors as miners' leaders used the language of conflict, intrinsic to Continental Syndicalism. Tension and confrontation were encouraged by transformations in the coal industry that included the consolidation of local unions in south Wales into the South Wales Miners' Federation, centralised bargaining, the rejection of conciliation, affiliation to the Miners' Federation of Great Britain, and the development both of Syndicalism and of activity by the Independent Labour Party.

Economic conditions and developments encouraged a questioning of the ability of the system to solve disputes and pressure for an independent working-class political organisation. Strikes helped to radicalise the workforce. *Llais Llafur* ('Voice of Labour'), the first Welsh-language Socialist newspaper, appeared in 1897. Keir Hardie was elected for Merthyr Tydfil in 1900, the year in which the Labour Representation Committee, the basis of the Labour Party, was founded. This showed that Labour was emerging as a potential challenger to the Liberal Party in Wales. That challenge was effectively resisted in the years down to 1914, a period of, at least in part, Liberal–Labour co-operation, where Socialism was conceived of in sectional terms and therefore alien to the wider community ethos. However, the decision of the south Wales miners in 1906 to affiliate with the Labour Party marked the beginning of the end of Liberalism's hold over the Welsh working class. By 1910, there were five Welsh Labour MPs.

That year, fresh industrial disputes reflected the downward pressure on payments caused by more difficult economic circumstances. Disputes in the coal industry arose from pressure on the profitability of pits and on miners' living standards, due in part to geological factors which reduced pit productivity. Employers tried to restrict customary rights and payments: coal prices and hence wages were determined by individual mine owners at the Coal Exchange Building in Cardiff. The coal industry was affected by shifts in the pattern of demand: the problems of the iron industry were important, and the new manufacturing processes for iron and steel consumed less coal. South Wales exported most of its coal, providing about 30 per cent of British coal exports in 1870 and 40 per cent of the much greater total in 1910. Welsh coal was particularly useful for steam-raising. Cardiff was the great coal export port, followed by Newport and then Swansea. South Wales was therefore affected by the rise in foreign competition, particularly from the USA, which became the largest world producer before the First World War, as well as from Germany and Belgium. Furthermore, the British industry did not match these rivals in adopting mechanisation in coal-cutting and transport.

As a result, labour remained the crucial cost, and problems led to pressure to cut labour costs by sacking miners or cutting wages. This encouraged confrontational industrial relations. A new more adversarial and combative working-class consciousness developed. The Cambrian Combine strike of 1910–11 began in September 1910 in a dispute over pay rates for starting up difficult seams at the Eli Colliery. Sabotage by striking miners in 1910 against collieries, strike-breakers and the trains attempting to bring them in, as well as extensive looting, were resisted and led to much violence. At Tonypandy, where the strike was a demand for social change, a miner was killed by police on 17 November, and troops were sent in by the Home Secretary, Winston Churchill, to enforce order, although he held them back and was criticised for allowing the rioters to destroy property. The strike ended in August 1911 with the miners defeated.

That year, a rail strike led to sabotage at Llanelli, and again to the deployment of troops, who shot two demonstrators dead. The social fabric was under great strain, and looting expressed both desperation and anger. As with other such disputes, there was a potent mixture of workers dissatisfied with specific conditions and others seeking political transformation. Thus, in south Wales in the early 1910s, Syndicalists advocated public ownership

(Communists followed suit after 1918). *The Miners' Next Step*, a Syndicalist work of early 1912 published in Tonypandy, was in favour of direct action and social change, based on a revolutionary miners' union. It should be noted, however, that industrial militancy in Wales in the late Edwardian period was neither continuous nor, in most of Wales, deep-seated. The end of the minimum wage strike in May 1912 led to a reaction against Syndicalist-inspired militancy. Liberal–Labour co-operation remained ascendant in the years before 1914, even in such places as the Rhondda. The personalisation of capitalism that stemmed from the role of individual mine owners helped create a particular kind of community politics in Edwardian Wales wherein Socialism was viewed in sectional terms. Before the Great War, despite the strains focused by Syndicalism, the community ethos of Liberal–Labour prevailed.

Although there was a major strike in 1915, industrial and political militancy receded during the First World War (1914–18), in part because the government brought peace to the coalfields by taking control in 1917. In 1919, however, Lloyd George rejected pressure from the miners for nationalisation. In 1921, the mines were returned to the coal owners and a major dispute, in which south Wales played a prominent role, lost by the miners; troops were deployed in south Wales. This was a very bitter aftertaste for the suffering of the First World War.

The war led to heavy casualties among Welsh troops. Wales provided a higher proportion of recruits per head of population than England, Scotland or Ireland. Yet there was also a significant anti-war movement drawn from a Nonconformist minority and from left-wing groups. Wales shared in the impact of the conflict. The human cost was exacerbated by conscription, a controversial measure which was introduced in 1916. The extension of government control over the economy was also important, as was the added economic demand caused by the war. This affected mining, manufacturing and agriculture, producing, for example, a markedly increased demand for cereal crops. The percentage of tillage rose by over 40 per cent throughout Wales. The war also led to an expansion in the public role of women, especially in industry. Combined with a sense of a shift from the pre-war political agenda, this encouraged the granting of the vote to women. In 1918, the vote was extended to women of 30 and over, as long as they were householders or the wives of householders; for men, the voting age was lowered to 21 and there were no comparable restrictions. The new electorate, which in

Wales had expanded by over half, rewarded Lloyd George and his Coalition government with a thumping victory in the general election of that year. Of the 36 seats, 20 were gained by Coalition Liberals, 4 went to allied Conservatives, and 1 to an allied Labour 'National Democratic Party'. Only one Asquithian (opposition) Liberal was elected, although Labour gained 10 seats on 30.8 per cent of the votes cast. Lloyd George had persuaded the chapels to throw in their lot with the war effort, but the First World War was effectively the end of an age of innocence in Wales. The old Nonconformist nostrums never quite worked thereafter.

INTERWAR WALES

Interwar Wales was affected by similar trends to the rest of Britain's, for example the rise of the automobile, or of radio, which began in Wales in 1923. However, they played out in a society that was particularly hit by the crises in mining and heavy industry. Depression in the coal industry led the employers to cut wages in 1926 and 1931, and union resistance was unsuccessful. Nevertheless, thanks to labour disputes in the coalfield, Glamorgan was the most strike-prone British county in the interwar period, whether the criteria is the number of strikes, the number of strikers, or the working days lost.

Meanwhile, based on south Wales, the Labour party was becoming more prominent, taking 10 Welsh seats in 1918 and 25 in 1929. This was the new Wales that followed the First World War: an increasingly fluid society with different suppositions and loyalties to those of the pre-war years. Disestablishment was finally achieved in 1920 and Wales gained an Archbishopric at St Asaph. This laying to rest of old animosities helped prepare the way for an age that was more secular in temper and tone. Similarly, the role of the landed elite declined markedly, not least because of the major sale of estates in 1918–22: more than 25 per cent of Wales changed hands in those years alone. Tenant farmers bought most of the land, becoming freeholders in the process. More land followed in 1924-5. This led to a very different rural society, one in which deference played a scant role. This affected politics, hitting both Conservatives and some Liberal interests, which worked to the benefit of Labour.

More generally, Welsh Liberalism was affected by the same problems that led to the rapid national decline of the divided Liberal party in the 1920s. Lloyd George's alliance with the Conservatives proved ultimately destructive to the Liberal party, not the Conservatives. Instead, the latter benefited from a unifying of anti-Socialist forces. Thus an anti-Coalition Conservative won the by-election in Newport in October 1922 that helped precipitate the fall of the Lloyd George coalition. Lloyd George's popularity also suffered from disquiet in Wales about particular policies, not least attitudes to the Irish crisis, while his integrity also became an issue. He nevertheless remained popular in Wales until his death in 1945.

Labour benefited more than the Conservatives from the Liberal crisis in the 1920s. Local, by- and general elections registered Labour's advance, especially in the south Wales coalfield where in 1922 the Liberals lost six seats to Labour. Only eleven Liberals and six Conservatives were elected, the former largely restricted to rural areas, especially to Welsh-speaking areas, the latter to coastal south-east Wales. The Liberals had lost their grip on the industrial and mining areas. This shift led to, and reflected, an increase in class-consciousness, and this was linked to labour disputes. In addition, there was a rise in Communist support, especially among the coal miners. This contributed to the bitterness surrounding and stemming from the national miners' strike in 1921. Branch meetings became more important than chapels as centres of working-class activity. The decline of the chapel as the centre of community life in Wales was itself particularly marked in the post-1918 period, and served to alter significantly the nature of Welsh society, Wales in essence becoming a more secular society as the pull of the chapel declined.

This was a Labour Wales that had to confront significant economic change including major decline in important and traditional industries. International competition, especially but not only from Germany and the USA, an overvalued pound after the return to the gold standard in 1925, inadequate investment and industrial problems hit the coal industry, and production fell heavily. This pressed on the living standards of miners, leading to a national miners' strike in 1926, in which south Wales took a major role. The locking out of the miners led to the Trades Union Congress calling a national strike known as the General Strike. This enjoyed massive support in the coal-mining regions, and very little backing in rural areas. The TUC did not wish to press the confrontation, and the strike was rapidly called off. Industrial disputes helped further to radicalise the miners in this period, and to encourage a sense of community in which distinctiveness and political and industrial militancy played a major role. After the failure of the General Strike in May 1926, the miners slowly went back to work, but continued support for the strike was strongest in south Wales. The South Wales Miners'

Federation estimated that only 3 per cent of miners had gone back to work by early November. The comparable figure in the Midlands was over half. The Federation and its leaders were more militant, even revolutionary, than the Midlands counterparts. Nevertheless, in December 1926 the miners returned on the employers' terms.

The following year, Welsh miners staged a march to London to demonstrate their plight. This brought no benefit. Conditions in the coalfield remained dire and, in some respects, became more so as a result of the 1931 Schiller award on mine wages. The failure of the General Strike left the Federation weak and its membership fell by over half in 1925–32.

The iron and steel and tinplate industries were also badly hit by economic decline. All the Cardiganshire lead mines were closed by 1931. The number of operating quarries in Caernarvonshire fell from 45 in 1897 to 14 in 1937. Welsh unemployment rose from 13.4 per cent in December 1925 to 27.2 per cent in July 1930, and a peak of 37.5 per cent in 1932 (with Glamorgan and Monmouthshire having a rate of over 42 per cent), and despite the recovery of the mid-1930s was still 22.3 per cent in 1937, with the highest percentages that year in Brecon and Pembroke. The unemployment rate was higher than in England. Unemployment put very heavy burdens not only on the unemployed but also on the ratepayers supporting the Poor Law Boards of Guardians. Furthermore, the unemployment figures were a less than full account of unemployment and underemployment.

The industrial areas were worst hit by unemployment, but virtually all of Wales was adversely affected. The effects of unemployment were gruesome in the extreme where it hit hard, and for older people in south Wales the Depression is still a watershed experience. Unemployment led to a measure of government economic assistance with the South Wales Special Area designated in 1934, but this was far less than was to be the case after the Second World War. Furthermore, some of the assistance was of dubious value. Subsidies led to the development of Richard, Thomas and Baldwin's integrated steel-making plant at Ebbw Vale, but this inland site which began production in 1938, although close to coal, was distant from the cheap iron ore supplies of the east Midlands where location would have made more economic sense. Establishment of the Special Area could not prevent a rise in unemployment in 1935–6.

Wales benefited little from the economic growth of the 1920s and 1930s, in large part because it had missed out on the early stages of the boom industries of the period: electrical and mechanical engineering, cars and other consumer goods. The gross output in both electrical and mechanical engineering was well below that of any other region of Britain bar south-west England. Thus, a poor inheritance – of limited engineering skills and little investment – did not change. Limited growth in new industries ensured that new jobs were not created to replace lost ones, and it helped to keep the labour market relatively rigid. For example, the percentage of women in work remained below the national average.

The scale of the economic problems which Wales faced between the wars was such as to raise doubts about its ability to overcome them. There was indeed a remarkable degree of fatalism about the future prospects of Wales from within and without in the 1930s. In 1935, Thomas Jones asked *What's Wrong with South Wales?* The situation seemed desperate and remedies futile. Maybe the famous coalfield should become an open-air museum to an age long gone, 'a grand national ruin', whose inhabitants were moved to Hounslow or Dagenham in the booming south-east of England. In 1939, there was a proposal from the interventionist pressure group Political and Economic Planning to close Merthyr, for the good of its people and the British tax-payer, and to move its inhabitants to the coast of the Monmouthshire Usk

Valley. Such views illustrated the depth of the problems facing Wales after the collapse of the coal-mining industry. The 1920s and 1930s have been described by the distinguished historian of modern Wales, Kenneth O. Morgan, as 'locust years'.

Unemployment encouraged emigration, both overseas and within Britain to areas of economic growth, especially south-east England. This interacted with the more long-term trend in which many able and ambitious Welshmen pursued their careers in England, particularly London. Aside from Lloyd George, another good example is provided by the poet Dylan Thomas (1914–53). Born in Swansea and educated at Swansea Grammar School, he became a reporter with the *South Wales Daily Post* in 1931, but moved to London in 1934 to pursue his career as a poet and literary journalist. He was to move back to Wales in 1938, but maintained links with London.

Not everything was in economic decline in Wales. Deeside benefited from industrial growth in both steel and chemicals, the coastal towns of north Wales had some modest expansion, and the electric power system spread. In 1931, the North Wales Power Company, erected an overhead line across the Menai Straits and across Anglesey. Earlier steam-generating electricity power stations were closed. The anthracite coalfield in west Glamorgan did better than the steam and bituminous coalfield further east, and exports of anthracite contributed to the prosperity of Swansea which also benefited from the movement of oil for the refinery opened at Skewen in 1921. Cardiff and Barry, in contrast, were in a far more difficult position. There was prosperity as well as poverty. Alongside the strength of the General Strike in south Wales in 1926 there were also volunteers against the strike. The 6,830 recorded for Glamorgan made it the third most enthusiastic British county. By 1934 there was one cinema seat for every ten people in South Wales, and that year it was considered worth rebuilding the Olympia cinema in Cardiff, although the provision of cinema seats can be seen as an index of how dreadful life outside the cinema was.

However well individual areas and industries did, decline in particular industries such as coal mining affected much of the Welsh economy, while unemployment and poverty sapped much of the population, leading to malnutrition and poor housing. Much of the population lacked adequate food, clothes, housing and sanitation, and they were frequently cold and wet. Public health was badly hit and tuberculosis became a more serious problem. About 430,000 Welsh emigrated between 1921 and 1939, mostly to expanding regions in south-east England and the Midlands. Some of this was helped by the Ministry of Labour, not least movement to the new industrial centres of Dagenham, Hounslow and Slough. Many Welsh communities, such as Merthyr, had a net loss of population, leading to a sense of disruption, dislocation and bitterness both for those who left and for those who stayed behind. The elderly were the least mobile. The Earl of Plymouth, President of the National Industrial Council of Wales and Monmouthshire established in 1932, declared in 1938, 'the problem of the Welsh industrial areas will never be overcome until we have succeeded in finding a solution of the difficulties which confront our great basic trade, the coal trade . . . to achieve a balanced state in industry . . . essential we should have light industries'. Neither solutions to the problems of coal nor light industries were to be forth-coming in the interwar period. Indeed the coal industry remained undercapitalised, with little investment in new machinery. Furthermore, the competition from oil became more important. The Welsh collieries, which had employed 272,000 men at the beginning of 1920, had only 126,000 miners by 1934.

Alongside Labour dominance, these were also years of growing activity on the part of nationalists. Plaid Cymru, the Welsh Nationalist Party, was formed at a meeting at a temperance hotel during the Pwllheli eisteddfod in August 1925 to campaign for self-government, but it had little impact. The party had only 500 members in 1930. Its 'back to the land' policy extolled agriculture and sought to obtain cultural and economic integrity and political autonomy. The party was concerned primarily with the Welsh language and opposed to urban and industrial society and trade unionism, goals that were not shared by the bulk of the Welsh population. Furthermore, the idea of home rule was less potent and popular than at the close of the previous century. Keir Hardie had supported home rule and there was interest in federalism in 1919–20, but neither led anywhere. Not only was self-government for Wales a minor issue in the interwar period, but institutions for distinct administration also made far slower progress than that for Scotland. The Secretaryship of State for Scotland, last held in 1746, was revived in 1895; and in 1934, the Scottish Office was created in Edinburgh. The Welsh equivalents were not created until 1964, although a separate Welsh Department of Education had been created in 1907 and other devolved executive departments, such as the Welsh Board of Health (1920), thereafter. In 1941, Councillor George Williams of Cardiff, Chairman of the National

Industrial Council, complained that that body was 'the only organisation which can speak for the whole of the local authorities of the Welsh region on economic affairs'.

Government economic assistance existed, especially for the establishment of factories in 'special' areas designated in 1934, but was modest by comparison with the situation after 1945. The Treforest trading estate established in 1938 north of Cardiff employed only 2,500 workers in September 1939. The modest level of intervention in the economy led to criticism by a group of radical young Conservatives, such as Harold Macmillan, and more loudly in Wales by Labour politicians such as Aneurin Bevan and James Griffiths. It contributed to a powerful sense of neglect and anger, almost betrayal.

The severely depressed economy of interwar Wales, keen on financial support from the national exchequer, was not the best basis for widespread demands for home rule. Furthermore, radicals in the 1930s did not tend to look to constitutional reform. Thus from 1933, Communist and left-wing Labour activists in the 'Little Moscows' of Wales such as Maerdy in the Rhondda, proposed the formation of workers' defence groups or militias on Continental lines, to resist police activity, which was generally seen as hostile. At Trelewis in 1935 the police clashed with miners in a serious confrontation.

Some elements in Plaid Cymru looked to Mussolini and were denounced as neo-fascists. An influential member, the poet Saunders Lewis, President from 1926 until 1939, was a neo-fascist. He was imprisoned in 1937 for an arson attack on an RAF base in Caernarvonshire. Indeed Welsh nationalism led Plaid Cymru, or at least its leaders, to oppose Britain's role in the Second World War (1939–45), which was seen as a clash of rival imperialisms. Some of its members were pacifists, products of a strong strain in Welsh nonconformity, others refused to be conscripted, and several – Arthur Owens and his group – may have been German spies and saboteurs.

Wales, again, suffered from the world war, although renewed economic demand helped cut unemployment. There was much wartime hardship. A large number of troops were killed during the conflict. In addition, German bombing brought death to the civilian population. Swansea was bombed from German bases in Brittany 44 times in 1940–43, most heavily in February 1941: 1,238 people were killed or wounded and over 7,000 made homeless. The destruction of the old town centre was followed by postwar rebuilding, much of it unattractive. Cardiff was also badly hit.

Nevertheless, the war was seen as a necessary struggle, far more so than the First World War had been.

Resistance to Hitler chimed with the views of the over-whelming majority of the Welsh labour force and there was little opposition to the war, especially after Hitler attacked the Soviet Union in 1941, ending the pact between the two powers which had affected Welsh Communists.

During the war, there was a strengthening of Socialist attitudes in Wales, and an emphasis on communal effort. This was less important in south Wales, where both were already strong, than elsewhere in Wales. State direction of resources and planning during the war also prepared the way for postwar nationalisations by Labour. A National Coal Board, for example, was created. Labour's major role in the coalition government from 1940 was also important in making the party seem a natural party of government.

Peace in Europe was followed in 1945 by a general election in which Labour won its first overall majority, a striking tribute to the unpopularity of what the Con-ervatives were held to stand for. Labour took 25 of the Welsh seats on 58.5 per cent of the poll. This was just over 10 per cent more than the overall Labour percentage for the United Kingdom. Wales had affirmed a Labour identity comparable to that of the Liberals in 1906. This included an unopposed election in Rhondda

West, and a majority of 34,000 in Llanelli, the largest in the UK. The Liberals held only seven seats. The new Labour government was determined to put the 1930s behind it and to build a new Britain and within Britain a new Wales.

POSTWAR WALES

The hardship of the interwar years was to help cement an identity of Wales and Labour that persisted in the postwar decades of economic growth. Whereas Lloyd George was the dominant Welsh figure in British politics in the opening decades of the century, in the 1940s and 1950s this role was assumed by Aneurin Bevan, MP for Ebbw Vale, a radical Socialist who played the key role in the foundation of the National Health Service and was no Welsh separatist. Labour enjoyed a degree of electoral support greater than that of the Liberals during their heyday. Wales was greatly affected by the nationalisation policies of the postwar Labour governments of Clement Attlee (1945–51). Coal was nationalised in 1947, the railways in 1948, and iron and steel in 1951. As a result, state planning became far more important to the Welsh economy. State control proved a means by which national investment flowed into Wales. There was extensive investment by the National Coal Board, especially in mechanised coal-cutting equipment, hydraulic pit props, and power loading. Services such as electricity were brought up to national standards, so that all properties requiring it were connected.

Along with Bevan, the Attlee governments contained another Welsh politician of note, James Griffiths. Griffiths served as Minister of National Insurance and, as such, completed the work which Lloyd George had begun nearly forty years before. It would thus be no exaggeration to say that the Welfare State in Britain bears a strong Welsh imprint.

Labour policies had other effects on the social politics of Wales. Taxation hit the great estates, a trend that had begun in 1920, and their decline influenced the society, economy and politics of rural areas: small freeholders became much more important. Stately homes sank into decay and many were demolished, Thomas Johnes's neo-Gothic Hafod in 1955.

Economic growth in the late 1940s did not bypass Wales, as that in the 1930s had largely done. Aside from growth in traditional heavy industries, such as steel and coal, there was also a development in light industry. Economic policy was far more active than in the 1930s and it brought results. New factories were constructed in depressed towns such as Merthyr and the skill-base improved and became more adaptable. Output rose more rapidly in Wales in 1948–54 than in Britain as a whole, although this owed something to earlier problems. Unemployment came close to disappearing.

Nationalisation produced investment, but could not remedy the long-term problems of an economy in which the single most important form of employment – coal mining – was a diminishing asset. Furthermore, the problems of the industry had a wider impact, especially in the economy of south Wales. Thus, for example, strike rates in Wales remained well above the national average in 1946–73 because of disputes involving the pits. Yet, even when mining was excluded, Wales was the region that was most affected by strikes. This owed a lot to a general culture of militancy, but also owed something to the units used, as when smaller regions were employed the most strike-prone part of Wales in the period – the western Valleys of industrial south Wales – was less disrupted than Merseyside, Glasgow, Furness and Coventry. This disaggregation also revealed that north and central Wales had rates below the national average. The particular characteristics of the south Wales economy and political culture that encouraged high strike rates lasted until the collapse of the miners' strike in 1985. The continued militancy of the south Wales miners showed in the area strike ballots of December 1971, February 1974, November 1979, January and October 1982 and March 1983 in each of which the vote for a strike was above the national average, most markedly in October 1982 (59 per cent to 39 per cent) and March 1983 (68 per cent to 39 per cent). In 1984, there was no ballot before supporting the coal strike: traditions of industry militancy and Socialism interacted with strong local concerns about pit closures and unemployment. The situation in north-east Wales was very different. Only 32 per cent voted for a strike in the area strike ballot in 1984, work continued during the dispute at Point of Ayr, and there was an important return to work at the Bersham pit in August 1984.

The continued dominant role of coal was not therefore a sign of strength in the late 1940s. However, at that point, demand was buoyant, and indeed the major problem was that of meeting it. Although production costs remained high, the 1950s saw investment and expansion in the coal industry. More generally, the prolonged boom in the Western economy between 1945 and 1973 helped underwrite policies of full employment that kept unemployment relatively low. Unemployment figures remained higher in Wales than in south England or the Midlands, but the percentage was low: 3.3 in

1964. Compared to the 1930s or the 1980s these were very good years. Regional development policies helped encourage factory-building. South Wales was designated a Development Area in 1945 and the Wrexham district in 1946. However, the situation became less promising from the late 1950s as competition from western Europe and then Japan increased, and as the staple industries encountered greater problems.

Wales remained a Labour stronghold until the 1960s, but only by varying its appeal, region by region. The nature of Plaid Cymru's appeal was illustrated by the adoption speech made by Gwynfor Evans in launching his parliamentary campaign in Merioneth in 1959,

> There is a great awakening in Merioneth and throughout Wales – the sound of chains and fetters breaking. Wales is experiencing an awareness of its nationhood, becoming proud of its ancestry, and gaining mental and spiritual freedom which will inevitably lead to national freedom . . . If we make a breach in this wall, we shall soon see the people following.

The electors, however, had little time for such rhetoric. Evans came bottom with 22.9 per cent, no real improvement on his performance in 1955. Despite an implicit alliance between the Conservatives and Liberals which led to the Conservatives not fielding a candidate, Labour held the seat. The seat was not to be won by Plaid Cymru until 1974. The party only won 69,000 votes in the 1964 general election: the Welsh electorate again preferred Labour. In the 1966 general election, the total Plaid Cymru vote was 61,000: 4.3 per cent of the total.

Meanwhile, devolved government for Wales had been created. There had been pressure for it in the late 1930s from Liberals and some Labour supporters. A Council for Wales and Monmouthshire was established in 1948, but it had no more independent power than the Ministry for Welsh Affairs created in 1951. In 1957, the government turned down the Welsh Council's suggestion that a Secretaryship of State for Wales be created. In the late 1940s, there had been a bitter internal debate in the Labour Party between James Griffiths and a critical Bevan over the creation of a Welsh Secretaryship and over devolution.

The Labour governments of Harold Wilson (1964–70, 1974–6) actively encouraged policies of regional development. Wilson established the Secretaryship of State for Wales in 1964 and appointed the respected James Griffiths to the post. A Welsh Economic Planning Board and an advisory Economic Council for Wales were also formed. Most of Wales became a Development Area in 1966 (the major exceptions were Monmouthshire and parts of Clywd) and in 1967 more incentives were offered with the Special Development Areas: much of Gwynedd and the south Wales coalfield. Also in 1967 Newtown was designated as a New Town to try to encourage economic activity in mid-Wales. The other New Town, Cumbran in south Wales, designated in 1949, was more conventionally an overspill town. In 1969, the areas covered in 1966 became Intermediate Areas. Investment and controls followed designation, although they did not bring increased economic efficiency or encourage the movement of labour which, while disruptive, might have been more beneficial in the long term. New industrial sites included the Anglesey Aluminium Company, which began smelting at Holyhead in 1971. This policy was given new energy after Labour returned to power in 1974. The Welsh Development Agency was founded in 1976, the Development Board for Rural Wales in 1977. The policy was cut back under the Conservatives, who gained power in 1972, although in 1984 much of south Wales was designated as Development or Intermediate Areas.

In 1966–8, there was an upsurge in support for Plaid Cymru, with their first parliamentary seat won by Evans at Carmarthen in a by-election in July 1966. At Carmarthen, Plaid Cymru provided an attractive alternative for those angered by national and local Labour policies. The party also benefited from the upsurge of nationalist feeling in Wales. The decline of the Welsh language was the proximate reason for this. Victory helped make Plaid Cymru credible and respectable: the impact of the Scottish National Party in the same period powerfully contributed to the same end.

In by-elections in 1967–72, Plaid Cymru also made an impact in English-speaking south Wales, doing very well in by-elections at Rhondda West in March 1967 and Caerphilly in July 1968. This upsurge owed much to the unpopularity of Labour's economic policies, and was a consequence of disillusionment with the Labour government of Harold Wilson, as well as a reaction against the self-interested and occasionally corrupt dominance of most of Welsh local government by Labour. Labour seemed stale. The closure of many collieries also lessened its popularity in south Wales. Unemployment again rose.

In the June 1970 election, Plaid Cymru contested all the Welsh seats for the first time, and won 175,000 votes, 11.5 per cent of those cast, but the first past the post system denied it any seats. Carmarthen was lost. Instead, Labour took 27 seats, the Conservatives, in an election that returned them to power, seven and the Liberals one. This was a serious blow to Welsh nationalism, but the Conservative government of Edward Heath (1970–4) failed to win any lasting support in Wales. Instead, the danger for third parties, as later in 1997, was that a swing against the Conservatives would essentially benefit Labour.

Nevertheless, devolution was becoming an important issue. The Kilbrandon Report in 1973 recommended a Welsh assembly with executive powers. In the next election, held in February 1974, Labour's share of the Welsh vote fell to less than half for the first time since the Second World War and they took only 24 seats compared to eight for the Conservatives, two for the Liberals and two (Caernarfon and Merioneth) for Plaid Cymru. Nevertheless, the party lost support in the south Wales coalfield and was largely restricted to rural Wales. This was accentuated in the election of October 1974 when there was the same distribution of seats with the exception of Plaid Cymru's capture of Carmarthen from Labour.

The Labour government was already pledged to a directly-elected Welsh assembly. A consultative document, *Devolution Within the United Kingdom: Some Alternatives for Discussion*, was published in June 1974 and a White

Paper, *Democracy and Devolution*, was published that October. The new assembly would sit in Cardiff and would have executive rather than legislative powers.

After the 1974 elections, Plaid Cymru's support dipped in the 1970s and 1980s, and when it revived, in the 1992 election, it did so in the Welsh-speaking heartland of Gwynedd and districts which were economically stagnant, and not elsewhere. Having taken 10.8 per cent of the vote in October 1974, Plaid Cymru gained only 7.6 per cent in 1979, losing Carmarthen. The 1983 and 1987 elections were not triumphs: in 1987 the party won only 124,000 votes, 7.3 per cent of the total cast.

In 1992, Plaid Cymru's vote rose, although its share of the Welsh vote was still 2 per cent below that in 1974, and it won a fourth seat – Ceredigion (Cardigan) and Pembroke North – from the Liberal Democrats. The five seats where Plaid Cymru's vote increased by 5 per cent or more were among the ten Welsh-speaking constituencies. In the top five of the latter, Plaid Cymru's vote was an average of 40.6 per cent (with a peak of 59 per cent in Caernarfon), but elsewhere its highest percentage was 15.6 per cent, and Plaid Cymru candidates lost their 23 deposits. Thus their geographical concentration enabled Plaid Cymru to win 0.6 per cent of the UK's seats with just 0.3 per cent of the votes, a striking contrast to the position of the Liberal Democrats, whose greater national vote was more evenly spread geographically (though not in Wales).

Plaid Cymru had more impact than its failure to move out of the Welsh-speaking heartland might suggest. Concern about its strength led Labour to establish a royal commission on the constitution in 1969 (which produced the Kilbrandon Report four years later), and then to support the idea of an elected assembly for Wales when it returned to power in 1974. Yet, this has to be seen as a parallel to the greater impact of the Scottish Nationalists. Scotland was more important to the Labour Party and the SNP were more powerful than Plaid Cymru.

A Scotland and Wales Bill introduced in 1976 proposed an assembly with control over health, social services, education, development and local government, but with no taxation power and with the Westminster Parliament retaining the veto. The Bill met opposition from nationalists who felt that it did not go far enough but, more substantially, from Labour politicians such as Neil Kinnock and Leo Abse, and Conservatives. The unattractive consequences of regional dominance in an autonomous Wales was stressed, as, conversely, was the danger of discrimination against non-Welsh speakers.

Conservatives regarded devolution for Scotland and Wales as a threat to Britain, and also saw the issue as a way to weaken the government. Much of the debate was similar to the *Cymru Fydd* dispute in the 1890s.

In order to secure the passage of the Bill, the government had to concede referenda, and, even then, the first Bill was defeated in February 1977. That November, separate Bills were introduced for Scotland and Wales and they passed the following spring. The referenda, however, were a different matter. Held on 1 March 1979, the Welsh referendum found only 11.8 per cent of the electorate in favour of devolution, with 46.5 per cent voting against and 41.7 per cent not bothering to vote. Even in Gwynedd and Dyfed, the overwhelming majority of those who voted did so against devolution, in the former case because they did not want to be run from distant Cardiff. The unpopularity of the Labour government of James Callaghan (who himself sat for Cardiff south-east) in its last months sapped support for devolution. The vote for devolution in Scotland was far stronger: it was a majority of the votes cast, but not of the electorate.

The ballot box was not the only medium in which the identity and future of Wales were contested. In February 1962, Saunders Lewis gave a radio broadcast '*Tynged yr*

Iaith' (*'The Fate of the Language'*) pressing for a firmer defence of the Welsh language. Arguing that this was more important than home rule, Lewis called for militant action. This led that summer to the launch of the Welsh Language Society, which sought to promote bilingualism. The bulk of its members were university students and the foundation of the Society marked the beginning of a more militant approach toward the protection of the native tongue. Direct action was the call and demonstrations were employed to force the use of the language. This could be seen as inspiring or selfish and destructive, and in practice was a mixture of both. The public life of Wales was obstructed for a cause. From 1963 the Society painted over English names on signs, organised demonstrations and undertook sit-ins. This might seem harmless, but other aspects of direct action were far less attractive. A radical fringe formed the Free Wales Army and this resorted to bombings with English-owned companies and holiday homes the targets.

The Wilson government responded to the new climate with the Welsh Language Act of 1967 which gave Welsh equal legal validity. It was followed by the establishment of the Welsh Language Board, first in 1988 as an advisory group by the Conservative government, and then in 1994 as a statutory body to promote the use of Welsh.

Nevertheless, the percentage of Welsh-speakers continued to decline: 40 per cent (1911), 30 per cent (1950), 25 per cent (1970) and, despite the teaching of Welsh in more schools, about 18 per cent in the 1990s. There were warnings that Wales would lose its language and become 'Welshless', with all that this would imply to a distinctive cultured tradition. The major communication developments of the century – radio, cinema and television – helped the English language seem the language of excitement and access. This owed much not to England but to the USA: American culture made English the universal language, but in Wales this had unintended consequences in linguistic use.

Welsh is spoken most in the rural areas that have been affected seriously by depopulation over the last century. The rural depopulation that affected much of Wales during the century, especially in the 1930s and after the Second World War, hit hardest in traditionally stable agrarian areas, many of which were Welsh-speaking, such as the Llŷn peninsula. In Anglesey, Welsh-speaking is lowest in most urban and coastal districts and strongest in the rural inland parishes, which have not been centres of population growth. More generally, the job opportunities provided in south Wales, England and abroad required fluency in English. The growth of tourism had the same effect. Practically all Welsh-speakers are bilingual. This does not imply that determined efforts were not made to keep the language alive and to link it with new media. This was true both of the development of Welsh television and of the growth of a Welsh pop culture in the 1960s. In the 1990s, bands from Wales, such as Catatonia and the Manic Street Preachers, were prominent in the British music scene. Even the veteran Welsh rocker Tom Jones was then considered cool. The use of Welsh and number of Welsh-speakers increased from 1981.

The use of the language is not the same as a loss of identity, although the latter is far from static: Welsh culture gets remade all the time. The religious life of south Wales remained Welsh-speaking even after Welsh ceased to be the common language. The English-speaking culture of south Wales is a Welsh culture: it's certainly not English. Just because they spoke English, it would be wrong to argue that major politicians such as Aneurin Bevan and Neil Kinnock were not Welsh. There was something of a struggle between Welsh-speaking and Anglo-Welsh proponents about cultural identity, and often both sides took up exclusionist standpoints in the 1960s and 1970s. In the case of Kinnock, Labour Party leader 1983–92, the fact that he was Welsh was in itself enough to make him, in the eyes of some, an unsuitable Prime Minister. He was labelled the 'Welsh boyo' by some sections of the British press.

Nationalist consciousness and pressure was not restricted to language. More violent nationalist groups used bombs to attack what they saw as alien bodies, such as reservoir dams and pipelines taking water from drowned Welsh valleys to English cities, a cause that had first led to violent action in 1952. In 1958, the contentious Tryweryn reservoir highlighted the powerlessness of Welsh public opinion to change parliamentary legislation. An entire community of people was displaced so that Liverpool could have adequate water supplies. This lent force to a change in attitude in which the union with England came to be viewed as a link forged and operated for the benefit of the English.

Until the outbreak of the 'Troubles' in Northern Ireland, Wales was considered the bigger internal security risk. A rise in sporadic terrorist activity in 1966–9, with large numbers of arson and bomb attacks, was followed in July 1969 by the investiture of Prince Charles as Prince of Wales at Caernarfon Castle after a crash course in Welsh. This metropolitan-inspired attempt to stabilise support for the Union in Wales succeeded in its aim. There was a marked decline in terrorist acts in the 1970s, as devolution seemed a serious prospect, but its failure and the unpopularity of the Conservative government under Margaret Thatcher elected in 1979 led to a fresh upsurge. In 1979–97, Wales was governed by a party which was in a very substantial minority there, and which was seen by many Welsh people as English. Arson attacks on houses bought by outsiders, usually owned as second homes by the English, began in 1979. Terrorist activity in no way compared with Ulster's and what was usually involved were little incendiaries in letters or the burnings of empty cottages. Estate agencies were also attacked. The security services responded firmly. They were fearful of parallels to the situation in Northern Ireland, and benefited from support from the national government. In 1980–2, there were widespread arrests as activists were subject to Special Branch surveillance. The arrests led to controversial court cases, and to disquiet about police tactics. Yet the militants were resorting to a terrorism that threatened a measure of destabilisation.

A campaign of public protest forced the Thatcher government to honour its promise to establish a Welsh-language television channel, yet another example of the extent to which Wales took a disproportionate share of national expenditure, although it could also be argued that Gwynfor Evans's threat to starve himself to death was a non-violent way to pressure the government into honouring its pledge to set up the channel. The new channel, S4C, began transmitting in 1982. It uses English subtitles on some of its more popular programmes. Language carries with it an emotional force denied most political issues other than religion, and, in the case of some people, a transfer of energy from religion can be discerned.

An emphasis on language also served as the basis for a partial account of the Welsh past, one in which the emphasis was on Welsh versus English, rather than divisions within the Welsh. This was to be taken further with the tourist industry's development of heritage sites in which the emphasis was to be on struggles with the English rather than internecine disputes.

Alongside the nationalist pyrotechnics, it is worth noting that the principal political shift in the late 1970s was the rise of the Conservatives, who won 11 seats on a swing to them of 4.8 per cent in 1979 and 14 in 1983. Although harmed by the unpopularity of aspects of Conservative government from 1979, the Conservatives continued to have a political presence far larger than that of Plaid Cymru. They took eight seats in 1987 and six in 1992, on 29.6 and 28.6 per cent of the Welsh vote respectively. There was no debacle in Wales comparable to the introduction of the Poll Tax a year early in Scotland, and the fusion of anti-English and anti-Conservative sentiment that was so bitter in Scotland was less so in Wales. There was no major swing against the Conservatives until the 1997 election. That the reaction against the Conservatives came later in Wales than in Scotland was primarily due to the influence of personality. Thatcher tended to appoint Conservatives who were One-Nation Tories to the Cabinet-ranked position of Secretary of State for Wales: Nicholas Edwards in 1979 and his replacement in 1987, Peter Walker (who held the office until 1990). Throughout the Thatcher years, then, Wales was a place apart enjoying considerable public investment and public/private partnership. Indeed, so keen was Thatcher to keep Walker in the Cabinet in 1987 that she agreed to let him run Wales his way. Walker would always support the general Thatcherite line in Cabinet but then add that Wales was a special case.

As in England, the Conservative party was no longer one of the shires. Indeed the suburban Conservatism that had been so important in England from the 1880s became more so in Wales. The rise in Conservative support was linked to social changes, not least the growth of a white-collar workforce for whom traditional loyalties had scant interest. This was a workforce living not in the Valleys but on the north and south coasts and in the Cardiff urban region. The interwar Labour advance in south Wales from the Valleys to the major towns was partly reversed. This reflected not only social change and the appeal to some of Thatcherite Conservatism, but also the extent to which the Labour Party appeared to have lost direction and become a complacent power system out of touch with social changes and developments in the economy. In part, this was unfair. There was considerable vitality in the Labour Party in Wales, but it was also affected by the problems of the Callaghan government (1976–9) and by the divisiveness and, in large part unpopular, radicalism that more generally affected Labour in the early 1980s.

Expansion in service industries and, in particular, in administrative agencies based in Cardiff, created much new employment, as did investment in new industrial plants. This investment was both from within Britain and from abroad. Indeed, south Wales proved particularly successful at attracting foreign investment, especially but not only from Japan and the USA. South Wales benefited more than any other part of Wales from Britain's entry into the European Economic Community in 1973, because much of the foreign investment was seeking a manufacturing base in the EEC. Depressed regions else-where in Wales received regional aid, but the resulting benefit was limited.

One major field of postwar investment was the chemical industry, linked in particular to the British Petroleum Chemicals plant at Baglan Bay, a major source of ethylene. There were also important chemical works further east, as at Llanwern. These coastal locations reflected the importance of petrol as a source for organic chemical manufacture. Wales was far less important for inorganic chemicals. Such investment passed mid-Wales by, and that was also the area with the lowest percentage employed in service occupations: in 1971, employment of males in administrative, professional and other service occupations was below 25 per cent in only three counties in England and Wales: Montgomery, Radnor and Carmarthen.

New industry was concentrated in south Wales, the economic importance of which was boosted by a new proximity to markets, thanks to the opening in 1966 of the Severn Bridge, which had been called for since the 1930s, and the extension of the M4 motorway. Under Peter Walker, Wales benefited from considerable public investment, in particular on road links; economic planning brought benefits. Transport improvements strengthened the links between south Wales and southern England. The InterCity 125, a high-speed diesel train capable of travelling at 125 mph, was introduced in 1976 on the Paddington to south Wales route. There was no equivalent improvement in rail routes within Wales, or between England and either north or central Wales. The M4 road axis was enhanced in 1997 when a second road bridge across the Severn was opened. This helped bring Cardiff closer to Bristol, not Bangor. Furthermore, economic expansion led to a measure of immigration. Cardiff had long had an important immigrant population, especially near the docks, and this became more pronounced in the urban areas of south Wales. Nevertheless, the percentage of New Commonwealth immigrants remained below that in most major English cities.

A new geography of wealth and employment greatly favoured Cardiff and, to a lesser extent, Bridgend, Newport, Swansea and Wrexham. High-technology activity and employment became important. Computer-related companies, many multinational in ownership, brought many jobs. Japanese and American employers were particularly important, for example Sony and Sharp. Their location reflected the multiple attractions of south Wales, a combination of improved communications, government aid, and the willingness of the new work force to accept co-operative working practices. This was a world away from the coalfield of the 1910s and 1920s with its ingrained industrial militancy.

Conversely, coal and steel were badly hit in the 1980s. The expansion of the late 1940s, in particular in the massive and modern Port Talbot steelworks opened in 1951, was succeeded by closures and massive layoffs. The Ebbw Vale steelworks closed in 1975–6 with many redundancies, the Shotton steelworks on Deeside following in the 1980s. Nationalisation had not solved the problem of high coal prices in a competitive environment. Furthermore, domestic competition became more acute; as first oil and nuclear power and then natural gas came to provide a greater share of energy needs, both industrial and domestic. Gas was no longer produced from coal. The coal industry was badly hit by the falling real price of oil in the 1960s and, from the late 1960s, by the development of North Sea gas and oil production: and thus gas and oil that did not need to be imported. Successful national strikes by miners in 1972 and 1974 raised their wages, but also the cost of production, and by 1983 the south Wales pits were not profitable. Closures accelerated after the unsuccessful 1984–5 national strike, in which south Wales had again proved a militant area, and by 1986 only 17 mines were left in

Wales: there had been 28 in south Wales in 1984. By 1992 there were fewer than 1,000 miners in Mid-Glamorgan. The near-wholesale disappearance of the coal industry was a major transformation not only in the economy of south Wales but also in the life of many Welsh localities. The decline of the coal industry owed much to its uncompetitiveness in a energy sector that was increasingly competitive, but government policies were also important, not least in investment and pricing decisions. The lack of sympathy of the Thatcher government for the miners was significant in the fate of the coal industry.

The decline of coal did not only have an effect on the mining communities. It also hit related industries and services. For example, Cardiff had been one of the ten top British ports by value of exports in the late nineteenth century and up to the Second World War. In the interwar period Swansea had been in the same league, indeed it was more important. Exports from Cardiff were overwhelmingly dominated by coal and from Swansea by iron and steel products and coal. In the 1980s no Welsh port featured in the top ten. The problems of the traditional employment base ensured that unemployment figures were higher in the recessions of the early 1980s and early 1990s than they were across most of southern

England. In October 1984, every county in Wales had a rate of over 10 per cent and for all bar Powys and south Glamorgan it was over 15 per cent. Such figures brought with them heavy social problems, including depression, alcoholism and family breakdown. Poverty was also linked to poor health.

Economic decline had already left large areas of derelict land, 8,227 hectares of disused spoil heaps, 3,090 of disused mineral workings and 7,567 of disused buildings and installations in 1957. The Aberfan disaster, in which an unstable spoil-heap engulfed a school in 1966, killing 116 children and 28 adults, indicated the price of early industrialisation paid in the mid-twentieth century.

Restoration of the Valleys and countryside was another consequence of the virtual disappearance of the coal mines: the south Wales coalfield is now a tourist attraction, rather than the centre of a productive industry. The decline of the coal industry in Wales has been mirrored by the decline of the national rugby team since the glory days of the 1970s. There could be a link, as rugby was the long-time game of the mining communities of the Rhondda Valley. Despite the cushioning of social security, economic problems had a serious impact on the social framework. Average annual household income in Wales in 1991–2 was £22,015: lower than in the north of England or Scotland, but that concealed major regional and social variations and these were reflected in Wales's politics.

Much poverty was rural, and income levels in much of Wales were below EEC norms in the 1990s. It was difficult for women to obtain paid work in many rural areas. Hill farming was economically precarious and sensitive to price swings, especially for lamb. Furthermore, the nature of much of the terrain was less conducive to mechanisation than on the lowlands. Nevertheless, thanks in large part to mechanisation, the agricultural labour force fell in number. Pressure on farm incomes encouraged both migration to the cities and a measure of amalgamation of holdings. Despite this, the percentage employed in agriculture remained relatively high. In 1971 there were only four counties in Britain where more than 30 per cent of the male workforce was involved in agriculture. Two were Welsh: Montgomery and Radnor, as was one of the three in the 20–30 per cent group: Cardigan. The national average was under 2 per cent. A similar contrast was apparent in mining and quarrying. Rural poverty and inaccessibility were largely responsible for continued relatively high mortality figures: the number of deaths in the first year of life per 1,000 live births remained over 40 in 1951 in six counties of England and Wales. Five were in Wales: Anglesey, Radnor, Caernarvon, Merioneth and Monmouth. However, improved medical care stemming from the creation of the National Health Service, improved transport and better social welfare, helped cut infant mortality rates substantially, so that in 1980 they were below those in England.

Wales was affected by the same social trends as the rest of Britain and Western Europe. Secularism reduced the impact of religion and the Churches. Adult Sunday church attendance figures for 1979–84 revealed a very different situation to that in 1851, with no county having a rate of 20 per cent or more. The lowest figure was for Mid Glamorgan. Church membership figures also fell. This was linked to a rise in individualism that gathered pace from the 1960s. Traditional social assumptions were widely challenged. Thus the nuclear family as the normative basis for the household became less common. Divorce became more frequent, as did one-parent families. Women ceased to be seen largely in terms of family units – as daughters, spinsters, wives, widows and mothers – and, instead, benefited greatly from a major increase in opportunities and rights, and from a wholesale shift in social attitudes and expectations. Female employment rose spectacularly in Wales in the 1960s and 1970s, but most of it was low-paid.

The rise of individualism can be related to that of consumerism. They were not co-terminous, but had their focus on the individual – as a social entity and as a purchaser. This challenged earlier patterns of behaviour and classification. Instead of seeing people in class terms, it became harder to regard them as subordinated to the group. Thus, in terms of sexual behaviour, there was a new-found public awareness of homosexuality, while in religion worshippers were ready to choose among a variety of Christian (and non-Christian) beliefs. This was, in part, a rejection of the past – the 'I am a Baptist because my parents were Baptists' tendency – that was more generally a feature of society. The rejection of the authority of the past was most acute in the case of youth: parental attitudes, lifestyles and expectations were dismissed or otherwise overthrown. This was central to the fluidity of Welsh society in the closing decades of the twentieth century. It was not that earlier generations had not moved in search of work, changed their creed or switched vote, but rather that the rate and intensity of change was now higher and there was a greater willingness to see change itself as good and as a goal.

Change interacted with existing practices, not least in politics. Wales, like Scotland, is a four-party system. With 54.7 per cent of the vote in 1997 (49.5 per cent in

1992; 45.10 per cent in 1987), Labour was by far the largest party, much more so than in Scotland (39 per cent in 1992), but the amount of support enjoyed by the other parties was also important. Conservatives and Liberal Democrats had 32 per cent in 1997 (41 per cent in 1992; 47.5 per cent 1987), and were thus greatly underrepresented by the first past the post system. In 1997, electoral unpopularity cost the Conservatives all their Welsh seats, although they gained 19.6 per cent of the votes cast in Wales. In the May 1999 Assembly election, in contrast, in which proportionality played a role in the twenty 'top-up' seats, the Conservatives took eight of the twenty, as did Plaid Cymru, compared to only one for Labour, and three for the Liberals (for the total figures see p. 236).

In the 1997 general election, Labour had taken 34 seats (85 per cent of Wales's parliamentary representation) and Plaid Cymru 4 (10 per cent). This made Plaid Cymru the second largest party in terms of seats although in votes it was the fourth largest, with 9.9 per cent. Plaid Cymru remained a party of little relevance in many constituencies, a major challenge to its description as a Welsh National Party. It was perhaps because of this that Dafydd Wigley began to speak of Plaid Cymru as the party of Wales in the 1990s.

In the 1997 election, the general unpopularity of the Conservative government of John Major interacted with a specific sense of grievance in Wales. The appointment of English Secretaries of State – John Redwood in 1993–5 and William Hague in 1995–7 – did not help. Nor did the transfer of powers from local authorities and locally-nominated bodies to quangoes appointed by the central government and heavily Conservative in composition. Redwood used Wales as a test-bed to show that ultra-'dry' policies would work, just as Peter Walker had used it to show that interventionist or 'wet' policies would work. With the appointment of Redwood, John Major brought the tradition of regarding Wales as a special case to an end. Redwood was an ardent Thatcherite who, in his two years at the Welsh Office, attempted to bring Wales into line with the rest of the United Kingdom. His preference for free-market solutions and limited government involvement undermined the credibility of the Conservative Party in Wales in the mid-1990s. It was Hague who witnessed the electoral destruction of his party in Wales in May 1997.

Conservative weakness continued to feature in the period of Labour ascendancy that began in 1997. This weakness helped Plaid Cymru to emerge as the most energetic opposition to Labour in the 1999 election. As a consequence, Wales increasingly diverged from the pattern of politics in England.

Although Plaid Cymru is not exclusively a Welsh-language party, and does not see itself as such, the problem that language creates for Plaid Cymru is indicated by the far greater degree of nationalist support in Scotland (21.5 per cent in 1992) where it is not an issue, compared to Wales (8.8 per cent in 1992) where it is possible to see the cause of the Welsh language, and Plaid Cymru's association with it, as divisive. From the perspective of, for example, Swansea with its Enterprise Zone near the M4, its retail parks and its new waterside developments, Welsh independence and cultural nationalism can seem a potentially dangerous irritant.

Yet this argument has to be handled with care. In the 1997 referendum, Swansea gave a majority vote for devolution. In the 1999 elections for the Welsh Assembly, the first democratically elected assembly in Welsh history, Plaid Cymru won both Islwyn and the Rhondda in the south Wales heartland of Labour. These were major inroads, and, conversely, there were some interesting Labour gains in Gwynedd. The issue of the Welsh language is now considerably less divisive than twenty years ago. A consensus around a compromise about the place of the language emerged in the 1980s.

The compulsory teaching of Welsh in schools has been accepted with relatively little opposition and the growth of Welsh-language schools in Anglicised areas is one of Wales's considerable success stories.

Wales, despite its relatively small size, is a very strongly regional country, and what goes on in Swansea has very little relevance, or is perceived as having little relevance, to what goes on in for example north Wales. Thus, the remote and sparse rural world depicted by the cleric and nationalist poet Ronald Thomas, as in *The Stones of the Field* (1946), *An Acre of Land* (1952) and *The Minister* (1953) is mentally distant from the cities of south Wales. In part, this is a cultural and political reassertion of the profound geographical differences which have always characterised Wales and which economic growth made even more central. The creation of Welsh agencies provided a new occasion for the voicing of regional anxieties. Thus, at the 1941 annual general meeting of the National Industrial Council of Wales and Monmouth-shire, Councillor G.O. Williams of Flintshire County Council emphasised that postwar reconstruction must be considered by two regional, not one united, committee, 'stressed the difficulties of travelling from North Wales' and declared that 'very little consideration had been given to the convenience of North Wales . . . a fatal step to have so few representatives of North Wales on the Reconstruction Committee . . . to justify the title of "national" it must have behind it the full backing of the whole of the people of Wales'.

Such regional differences are particularly apparent in Wales because of the language issue and everything that that represents and can be made to symbolise. Thanks to language, many of the Welsh are far more distinct from the English than the vast majority of Scots but, equally, the Welsh as a whole are – as the devolution vote in 1979, subsequent election results, and the very narrow majority for a Welsh assembly in the 1997 referendum (despite backing from Labour, Liberal Democrats and Plaid Cymru) revealed – far more likely to identify with a British future than are the Scots. Only 50.3 per cent supported devolution in Wales on 18 September 1997, compared to 74.9 per cent in Scotland a week earlier. The abstention of just under 50 per cent of the electorate in the Welsh referendum led to questions being asked about the legitimacy of the new assembly.

Eighteen months later, Tony Blair's use of the trade union bloc vote to ensure that his preferred candidate for the position of leader of the Welsh Assembly, Alun Michael, was elected, revealed a degree of central control inimical to the whole logic of devolution. The behaviour of the party's London leadership hit Labour's vote in Wales. Labour was expected to win an overall majority in the first elections to the new Welsh Assembly, but in the event narrowly failed to do so. The results of the elections, held on 6 May 1999, were as follows: Labour 28 seats, Plaid Cymru 17 seats, Conservatives 9 seats and Liberal Democrats 6 seats. Turnout was again disappointingly low, 46 per cent, and even fell as low as 30 per cent in some areas. The collapse of Labour's vote in its south Wales heartlands was the most marked feature of the elections; Labour lost the Rhondda, Islwyn, and Llanelli to Plaid Cymru. Labour's poor performance was attributed to grass-roots disillusionment with the party's 'Millbank tendency' and the imposition of Michael. Michael, who was elected as list ('top-up') member for Mid and West Wales, decided to form a minority Labour government. Unlike in Scotland, Labour did not need Liberal Democrat support, because both Plaid Cymru and the Conservatives agreed not to prevent Labour from governing without a majority; Plaid Cymru thus became the official opposition party.

If Wales follows a future within Britain, this will be a different Britain from that of the 1950s, or even the Unionism powerfully advocated by Mrs Thatcher. Such a shift is but part of a wider transformation in British society and political culture. The widespread erosion of deference has been linked to a lack of confidence in established ideas and institutions. This provides an opportunity for new beginnings, although it does not prescribe their form. Thus politics from the 1990s is playing a greater role in moulding the state than at any time this century, or indeed arguably at any time in the age of British mass democracy. This will lead to fresh debate about identities and interests, debate that requires an understanding of both the present and the past. The future position of Wales within the United Kingdom is now bound up with the success of the new Welsh Assembly. Its lack of legitimacy, given the level of turn-out in the 1997 referendum, is a problem. Not only must the Assembly be seen to be working for all the people of Wales, but all the people of Wales must be convinced that the Assembly is working for them. Plaid Cymru made much of the fact that Wales was only being offered an assembly with limited powers while Scotland had been offered a fully-fledged parliament of its own. If devolution, as many of its Welsh supporters intend, is a process rather than an event then the assembly may very well turn out to be a stepping-stone to a greater degree of autonomy in the future.

A federal Europe offers a possible alternative and Plaid Cymru make much of being good Europeans, arguing that they can campaign for European Union investment far more effectively than London-based parties. The regional dimension is currently on the European political agenda, as there is pressure for a movement back to smaller societies within a European framework. This comes particularly from political movements based on groups with a national consciousness, such as the Basques, the Catalans, the Scots and the Welsh, all of whom want their separate identities while remaining parts of Europe, the 'Europe of the regions'. The Council of the Regions has opened up avenues. Tourism, now Wales's leading industry, fortifies the Welsh's sense of history.

Yet the strongly regional nature of support for Plaid Cymru, combined with the divisive nature of the language issue, suggests that an autonomous Wales might well face an uneasy future: the different interests of south-east Wales and Gwynedd might be difficult to reconcile, although the Assembly's committee arrangements seem to address these. Different regional views are strongly present in the political system. A history of division might return and it would not be easy to blame this on the English. Much would depend on the electoral system. An autonomous Wales might resemble an England dominated by the demographic and economic weight of the south, but the degree to which this would be acceptable elsewhere in the two countries is unclear.

Yet this may be an overly pessimistic view. Alongside differences, there is an awareness of a living distinctiveness, as well as a greater degree of optimism than in England. This reflects both the extent to which Wales has not suffered a crisis of confidence from the collapse of the British empire but instead has enjoyed a process of political regeneration, and also the extent to which the bleak economic and social regime of the 1930s has been overcome. That remark is not intended to minimise recent and current problems and hardships, but there is nothing to match the misery and despair of the earlier period. This is a good background against which to chart the question of identity in the new millennium. For the present, the Welsh have an ability to pursue their different views without an excess of bitterness, while Wales has an attractive diversity that rewards both inhabitants and visitors alike.

LIVERPOOL LIBRARIES &
INFORMATION SERVICES

SELECTED FURTHER READING

Accessible recent studies include A.D. Carr, *Medieval Wales* (London, 1995), J. Gwynfor Jones, *Early Modern Wales, c. 1525–1640* (London, 1994), and Philip Jenkins, *A History of Modern Wales 1536–1990* (Harlow, 1992). Earlier and more detailed works can be found in their bibliographies, but it is particularly worth noting Wendy Davies's *Patterns of Power in Early Wales* (Oxford, 1990), Rees Davies's *Conquest, Coexistence and Change: Wales, 1063–1415* (1987), and Kenneth O. Morgan's *Rebirth of a Nation: Wales 1880–1980* (Oxford, 1981). Alongside these thoughtful general surveys there is a whole series of more detailed works. For example, the medieval period can be approached through James Given, *State and Society in Medieval Europe. Gwynedd and Languedoc under Outside Rule* (Ithaca, 1990), Ralph Griffiths, *Conquerors and Conquered in Medieval Wales* (Stroud, 1994), and Rees Davies's *The Revolt of Owain Glyn Dŵr* (Oxford, 1995). A visual dimension is offered by William Rees, *An Historical Atlas of Wales* (2nd edition, London, 1959). Cadw (Welsh Historic Monuments) have published a number of well-illustrated books, including, *A Mirror of Medieval Wales. Gerald of Wales and His Journey of 1188* (Cardiff, 1988) and Peter Gaunt, *A Nation Under Siege. The Civil War in Wales 1642–48* (London, 1991). Travellers' tales offer much of interest. Aside from Gerald of Wales, others of importance include Thomas Dineley, *The Account of the Official Progress of His Grace Henry 1st Duke of Beaufort through Wales in 1684* (1888), Thomas Pennant, *Tour in Wales* (1776), Hon. John Byng, *A Tour to North Wales* (1793) and Rev. W. Bingley, *A Tour round North Wales performed during the summer of 1798* (3rd edition, 1838). Interesting published correspondence includes Joanna Martin (ed.), *The Penrice Letters 1768–1795* (Cardiff, 1993).

INDEX

INDEX

INDEX